The Secrets of
Nostradamus
Exposed

Undisclosed mysteries of
"the world's greatest prophet."

D1559245

The Secrets of Nostradamus
Exposed

Undisclosed mysteries of
"the world's greatest prophet."

Ray Comfort

Living Waters Publications
California

Dedication: To my good friend and son-in-law Emeal Zwayne (EZ).

My special thanks to Gordon & Lori Anderson

Contents:

ISBN 1-878859-18-8

Library of Congress Catalog Card number: 96-94012

Ray Comfort
Living Waters Publications
P.O. Box 1172
Bellflower, CA 90706

Printed in the United States of America
February 1996.
Cover by Erik Hollander
Editorial assistance--Garry T. Ansdell.
The Secrets of Nostradamus Exposed
Ray Comfort

Foreword

Did Nostradamus predict the assassination of President Kennedy? Did he say that man would land on the moon, and that someone named Hitler would lead Germany? Did he mention America by name?

This publication will not only give you insight into the acclaimed prophecies of the world's most famous prophet, but it will show you *how* he obtained his predictions.

Some say Nostradamus was a man who heard from God. Others say his knowledge was obtained through the occult. This book will reveal to you that there was *another* means by which he obtained such incredible words.

Chapter One
Grave Consequences

The year was 1791. On a dark night in France during the height of the French revolution, three drunken soldiers took turns at digging a grave. They were about to exhume the remains of an acclaimed prophet, buried two centuries before. Legend said that whoever drank from the skull of the famed Nostradamus would inherit his magical powers. Legend also said that the same person would instantly die.

Fear had kept the grave undisturbed from those who had been tempted to try the cranium beverage...until that dark night in May, 1791.

After the intoxicated men lifted the half-rotten coffin out of the grave, they raised the lid to see a sight that paralyzed them with fear. Across the skeletal remains, held in the bony hands of the prophet lay a plaque which read "May 1791." Nostradamus, who had been buried 200 years earlier, *had predicted the very date of his exhumation*.

Undaunted by the plaque, one of the drunken troopers lifted the wine-filled skull to his quivering lips. *Suddenly he dropped to the ground*. A stray bullet from a riot during the revolution had been fired into the night, struck the man through the head, killing him instantly!

The Fog of the Future

The word "occult" means: *beyond human understanding...mysterious, secret, and hidden*. There has always been a mystery surrounding this incredible man named Nostradamus, both in his life, and in his death. How did he obtain his strange prophecies? What forbidden and bizarre practices did he perform in the secret of his study? Why did he conceal his writings and burn his books?

The occult is no longer a forbidden zone of human exploration as it was in the 16th Century. That which was taboo in the past has become part of the daily life of contemporary America. Almost every newspaper and magazine carries horoscope readings for their subscribers. Television parades celebrities who give enthusiastic testimonies about how they have been blessed by psychics.

What was once hidden in the closet has come out to even become part of the U.S. government. The CIA spent an amazing $20,000,000 on psychics from 1975-1995, in an effort to gain intelligence (*Time*, December 11, 1995). Even the wives of presidents have consulted psychics for guidance while in office.

At the beginning of each year, predictably, the news media parade a long line of those who profess to know the future. With hit and miss predictions, the procession moves from palm-reading to ball-gazing gypsies, to respectably dressed and clean-cut astrologers...all done in an effort to bring some sort of clue as to what the immediate hereafter holds for humanity.

In the thick fog of the future, now and then someone says something that actually comes to pass. Sometimes even the weather man gets it right.

Ball-shaped Dirt

Michel de Nostredame, better known by his Latinized name, Nostradamus, was a prophet who was never at a loss for words when it came to the future. While many have trouble remembering the past, he clearly saw the future.

The Secrets of Nostradamus Exposed

Most of us have a fascination for knowledge of coming events. If someone has cognizance of that which will take place, it hints strongly of some sort of Divine influence. It means that perhaps we are not alone on a ball-shaped lump of dirt, spinning through space. It means that if we can see that this man's prophecies were accurate in the past, we can rely on them to tell us what is about to take place in the future. That is a comforting feeling.

Jean-Charles de Fontbrune, the author of a number of books on the famous French prophet said of the fulfilled prophecies:

"The prophecy then becomes a source of comfort, a refuge for all those ordinary folk who have been sucked unwillingly into the whirlpool of conflicts over which they have virtually no control--or at least a strong defence case--for the existence of God, the Supreme Being. Throughout history, one of man's most enduring characteristics has been to acknowledge the existence of some force greater than himself." (*Nostradamus into the Twenty-first Century,* Jean-Charles de Fontbrune)

Nostradamus's parents celebrated the birth of their son on December 14th, 1503. In his early childhood, he went to live with his grandfather,

Jean, where he learned the classics and how to speak Latin, Greek and Hebrew. It was there that he developed skills in mathematics and astrology. His two grandfathers were personal physicians to the French King, and both encouraged his interest in astrology.

As years passed, young Michel studied philosophy, grammar and rhetoric under the eyes of Roman Catholic priests. He also cultivated his interest in the occult:

"In his free time he could be found in Avignon's renowned papal library sampling a wide selection of occultic and astrological books." (*Nostradamus and the Millennium*, John Hogue, Doubleday).

Nostradamus was born a Jew. However, the Roman church persecuted thousands of Jews from 1420-1498, calling them "the murderers of Jesus Christ." In the early 1500's, Louis VII ordered all Jews to be baptized as Catholics or "suffer the consequences," so the Nostradamus family decided to be baptized, but secretly held on to their Jewish beliefs. When Michel's father objected to his son's astrological activities, the grandfather suggested that the young man should become involved in herbal medicine, thus giving more credibility to his occult

15

activity. He was therefore sent to study at the University of Montpelier in 1522, where he amazed fellow students and teachers with his lectures on astrology. It was there that he was said to have expounded his teaching on the earth being round,

revolving around the sun, 100 years before Galileo. He graduated with his baccalaureate degree in 1525.

Nostradamus was not the sort of person who

would stand out in a crowd. "He was a little under medium height, of robust body, nimble and vigorous," wrote Jean Aymes de Chavigny, biographer of the prophet. "He had a large forehead, a straight and even nose, grey eyes which were generally pleasant but which blazed when angry and a visage both severe and smiling...By nature he was taciturn, thinking much and saying little, though speaking well in the proper time and place: for the rest, vigilant, prompt and impetuous, prone to anger, patient in labor."

Two-edged Sword

When the bubonic plague broke out in France, he tirelessly moved throughout the country among the sick, prescribing herbal cures, fresh air and fresh water. It was here that he gained a reputation as a "healer of afflicted ones," and was sent for by towns from all over Europe. It was his courage and his unusual, yet successful treatments which led to his initial recognition and following.

As his reputation grew as a doctor, so did his fame as a psychic. The nobles and the wealthy of his day began to frequent his home for their horoscopes.

In the mid 1530's, Nostradamus married and his wife bore him two children. Then in 1537, the plague visited his home town and tragically took his entire family. This had a two-edged sword. It not only tore his loved ones from his hands, but despite his success in other areas, because he couldn't cure his own family, it greatly damaged his reputation as a physician.

Idol Joke

Before the death of his family, Nostradamus made a casual but life-changing joke to a workman who was casting a bronze statue of the virgin Mary. He alluded to it in reference to the "casting of demons." This was later reported to church authorities, who called him to stand trial for what they considered to be heresy. Rather than face Roman Catholic Inquisitors, he fled east to Italy, avoiding the church for the next six years. It was during this time that his prophetic powers began to manifest themselves.

Ten years later, he returned to the town of Salon in France, where he settled for the rest of his life. Soon after, he married a rich widow named Anne Posart Gemelle. By day he lived as a "good Catholic," but by night he burned the candles as he consulted his ephemeris and delved into the mystics. He would empty his mind of all thought and gaze into a water bowl where he would see visions of the future.

After some time, he published an almanac which
became so successful, he marketed one each year
for the rest of his life.

Nostradamus planned for the future. He told a
friend that he would publish a book of the prophecies of mankind, that would tell of future events
until the end of time. The publication would be
called "The Centuries," made up of ten volumes,
each containing one hundred quatrains (a poem of
four lines) and totalling one thousand predictions.

He began his work on, *The Centuries* on Good
Friday of 1554, and soon after published the first
volume. Work on the publication was completed in
1558. Although he was praised by royalty, books
began appearing which condemned him as a con
man. His house was even stoned regularly by
zealous Roman Catholics.

As time passed, his writings became widely
known. Century 1, quatrain 35 warned:

The young lion will overcome the older one
One the filed of combat in single battle
He will pierce his eyes through a golden cage
Two wounds made one, then he dies a cruel death.

This was a prediction of the death of King
Henry, which is said to have taken place two years

after the prophecy was given. In the summer of 1559, the King was jousting with Montgomery, the

King Henry's fatal accident while jousting in 1559

captain of his Scottish guard. On the third encounter, the lance hit the King's armor, shattered, and a splinter entered the King's golden visor, going into his eye and then into his brain. Another splinter is said to have gone into his throat--"two wounds made one." He died an agonizing death ten days later.

This fulfillment of his words gave Nostradamus fame throughout all of Europe, promising a bright future for the prophet.

Chapter Two
Divine Origin

As with most people who have the gift of seeing into the future, Nostradamus was convinced that its source was Divine. He said of his inspiration:

"Although for a long time I have been making predictions of events which have come to pass, naming the particular locality, I wish to acknowledge that all have been accomplished through Divine power and inspiration."

His religious belief was that mankind, represented by Adam and Eve, fell from union with God into a state of forgetfulness. The way back was by studying the Tree of Life, a mystic path with ten levels of consciousness, similar to some eastern religions.

In March of 1949, Henry C. Roberts, the author

of *Complete Prophecies of Nostradamus*, speaks of the prophet's methods by saying:

"Beyond a shadow of doubt, the methods employed and results obtained by Nostradamus in looking into the future were outside of the physical framework.

"What to the contemporary critics of his day, for want of a better term they chose to call magic or occult, we today now recognize as the operation of certain tenuous and imponderable laws that permeate the entire Cosmos. These intangible but all pervading forces we group today under the general title of *Extra Sensory Perception*."

Author of the book, *Countdown to Apocalypse* Jean-Charles de Fontbrune goes even further and says:

"Nostradamus states once again: 'a small flame comes out of the solitude and brings things to pass which should not be thought vain'. Here he is alluding to the Holy Spirit, symbolized by the tongues of flame descending to the Apostles' heads at Pentecost."

In a letter addressed to his son, Nostradamus

again affirms that his prophecies came directly from God the Creator:

"...sometimes God the Creator by the ministers of His messengers of fire and flame, shows to our external senses, and chiefly to our eyes, the causes of future predictions, signifying the future event, that will manifest to him that prophesies. For the prophecy that is made by the internal light, comes to judge of the thing partly with and by the means of external light...The reason is evident why what he foretelleth comes by divine inspiration, or by the means of an angelical spirit, inspired into the prophetic person, anointing him with vaticinations..." (Ibid).

However, in Century One, quatrain one, Nostradamus gives details as to *how* he received his prophecies:

I sit at night alone in secret study
Resting upon the brass tripod:
A thin flame comes forth from the solitude
Making successful that which should not be believed in vain.

C1 Q2 reveals even more:

The divining wand in hand is placed in the

middle of the tripod's brass legs
With water he anoints the hem of his robe and foot:
Fear! A voice is heard. He trembles in his robes:
Divine splendor. The divine one sits nearby.

This method of obtaining prophecies had its foundation in a ritual practice by Branchus, an occultic Greek prophetess:

"Throughout these two quatrains Nostradamus was describing a variant of a divinatory magical rite...described by Iamblichus of Chalcis, who died about AD 335: 'The prophetess of Branchus either sits upon a pillar, or holds in her hand a rod bestowed by some deity, or moistens her feet or hem of her garment with water...and by these means...she prophesies.' This passage, which describes a divinatory rite involving the wetting of a foot and the hem of a garment, was clearly being referred to by Nostradamus..." (*Nostradamus*, Francis X. King, page 138-139, St. Martin's Press).

Nostradamus would sit on a brass tripod with his spine erect, using the fact that he was uncomfortable in that position, to remain alert. The tripod's legs were placed at the same degree angles as the pyramids of Egypt--this was supposed to create a bio-electric force which sharpened psychic powers. Another tripod was placed at his feet, filled to the brim with steaming water and stimulating oils. Then he would do incantations, after which he would do other things essential to the practice. He then tells what happens:

"I emptied my soul, brain and heart of all care and attained a state of tranquility and stillness of mind which are prerequisites to predicting by means of the brass tripod...the prophetic heat approaches...like rays of the sun casting influences on bodies both elementary and non-elementary...human understanding, being intellectually created, cannot see hidden things unless aided by a voice coming from limbo by help of the thin flame...from which comes a clouded vision of great events, sad and prodigious and calamitous adventures approaching in due time."

It is believed that this technique helped Nostradamus overcome a strong barrier of fear which came upon him before he surrendered his will in the occultic trance, of which he says:

"Although the everlasting God alone knows the eternity of light proceeding from Himself, I say

25

frankly to all to whom He wishes to reveal His immense magnitude--infinite and unknowable as it is--after long and meditative inspiration, that it is a hidden thing divinely manifested to the prophet by two means:...One comes by infusion which clarifies the supernatural light in him which predicts by the stars, making possible divine revelation: the other comes by means of participation with the divine eternity; by which means the prophet can judge what is given to him from his own divine spirit through God the Creator and His natural intuition."

Author Francis X. King said of his involvement in the occult:

"There is evidence to be found in the curious forty-second quatrain of Century One that makes it seem quite certain that Nostradamus had some knowledge of both the darker aspects of the occult arts and of modes of divination involving the use of bas-ins...That technique was described by the Neoplat-onic philosopher Psellus as follows: 'There is a type of predictive power in the use of the basin, known and practiced by the Assyrians...Those about to prophesy take a basin of water, which attracts the spirits of the depths. The basin seems to breathe as with sounds...The water in the basin...excels...

because of a power imparted to it by incantations which have rendered it capable of being imbued with the energies of spirits of prophecy...a thin voice begins to utter predictions. A spirit of this sort journeys where it wills, and always speaks with a low voice.'" (*Nostradamus*, Francis X. King, page 140, St. Martin's Press).

It is interesting that 3,000 years ago the Bible spoke of this spirit that "always speaks with a low voice":

"And they shall say unto them that have familiar spirits...that peep and mutter...and thy speech shall be low out of the dust, and thy voice shall be of one that hath a familiar spirit" (Isaiah 8:19, 29:4).

Royal Welcome
The story is told of Catherine de Medici, widowed Queen of France, visiting Nostradamus at midnight. In the flickering candle-light, he motioned her into a magic circle drawn on the stone floor. In front of the circle stood a mirror, upon which were inscribed four names of God written in pigeon's blood. Nostradamus then took the Queen's hand and began singing an incantation to an angel to stir the spiritual realm.

The apparition manifests before Nostradamus and Catherine de Medici, the Queen of France.

Suddenly, the image of the Queen's first son began to appear in the mirror and disappeared, signifying his coming death. Then an apparition of her second son appeared. It circled the room fourteen times, then disappeared, signifying that he would reign fourteen years before his death.

Finally, an apparition of her favorite son appeared and circled for fifteen times, then disappeared. The Queen was horrified that her beloved son would be taken after only fifteen years. Afterwards she asked the prophet if the mirror might have deceived them, but he insisted that it could not lie.

This incident is similar to an occurrence in the Bible (1 Samuel 28:7-14) where instead of a Queen, a *King* sought counsel through a psychic. King Saul contacted a familiar spirit through a medium, after vainly seeking God in prayer.

He said to his servants, "Seek me a woman that hath a familiar spirit, that I may go to her, and enquire of her."

After his servants found a woman, he disguised himself and went to her, despite the fact that it was forbidden under God's Law (Deuteronomy 18:11), and that the death sentence was proclaimed on anyone, man or woman, who had a "familiar spirit" (Leviticus 20:27).

During the meeting, an apparition was manifest similar to that seen by the Queen and Nostradamus, and spoke of the King's death. This came to pass a short time afterward.

Unger's Bible Dictionary (Moody Press) gives us insight into what a "familiar spirit" is:

"*...familiar spirit is a divining demon present in the physical body of the conjurer...The term "familiar" is used to describe the foreboding demon because it*

*was regarded by the English translators as a secret
("famulus"), belonging to the family ("familiaris"),
who was on intimate terms with and might be
readily summoned by the one possessing it."* (page
344)

On June 27, 1558, Nostradamus wrote a com-
prehensive letter to Henry II. In the epistle he
answers his contemporary critics as to whether or
not his prophecies were God-given:

"...Only the Eternal God, who is searcher of men's
hearts, being pious, just, and merciful, is the true
Judge of it; Him I beseech to defend me from the
calumny of wicked men...Notwithstanding those in
whom the malignancy of the wicked spirit shall not
be suppressed by length of time, I hope that after
my decease my work shall be in more esteem than
when I was alive."

The occult didn't have the respectability it has in
contemporary society. In his day, people were
burned for sorcery, so it was most necessary that he
convince the King that God Almighty was the sole
origin of revelation. He continues:

"...I confess truly, that all comes from God, for

which I give Him thanks, honor and praise, without having mixed anything of that divination...which proceeds not from fate but from God and nature."

Despite his pleas of innocence, Nostradamus was a "diviner." He used divination here described:

"In scripture the diviners were false prophets, and divination was allied to witchcraft and idolatry (Deuteronomy 18:10,18, Joshua 13:22, Jeremiah 27:9), energized by demon power (1 Corinthians 10:20-21)." Ibid .

Not the Authenticity

It is healthy to be suspicious of anything that proceeds from the occult. Blind faith is for the blind. We should "test all things, and hold on to that which is good."

If someone offers you quality merchandise at a suspiciously low price, you should not only ask if the merchandise is *genuine*, but also if it's stolen. If its source is the criminal world, then the second question is justified. The source of the French prophet's wares is obviously the underground of the spirit world. When the Bible speaks of a prophet doing signs and wonders, the question does not arise as to the *authenticity* of the miracle in ques-

tion, but as to its *origin*. The clear teaching of
scripture is that a supernatural manifestation is not
always an indication of the Divine presence. When
the Bible predicts the anti-Christ, it warns that he
will have "power and signs and lying wonders" (2
Thessalonians 2:9). This is further seen in Revelation 13:13-14, where he deceives those that "dwell
on the earth."

In Matthew 24:24, the Bible warns of false
prophets that will arise with "great signs and
wonders," causing great deception. What is the
deception?--the presumption that the signs are from
God. In the Book of Acts (Chapter 8:9), Simon
"bewitched" the people with his signs, yet his
power didn't come from God, it was demonic.

When the apparition appeared when King Saul
met with the woman who had a "familiar spirit," it
appeared "ascending out of the earth" and was only
seen by the woman. King Saul asked her, "What is
his form?" And she said, "An old man is coming
up, and he is covered with a mantle" (1 Samuel
28:14).

The lesson for us is not whether or not the
apparition was genuine, or whether or not the
prediction it made was true. The lesson is the fact
of the rebellion of King Saul in practicing witchcraft. The source of the apparition was demonic,

something so displeasing to God that He killed the King *because* he sought guidance from a familiar spirit:

"So Saul died for his transgression which he committed against the Lord, even against the word of the Lord, which he kept not, and also for asking counsel of one that had a familiar spirit, to enquire of it; and enquired not of the Lord; *therefore* He slew him..." (1 Chronicles 10:13-14, italics added).

Don't drink from a cool, clear stream until you have checked that there is not a dead, decomposed animal upstream a little. The question to ask is not whether or not the water you are drinking is genuine water. The question to ask is, what is the source...are the waters polluted?

We are easily deceived when we, like Saul, turn from God to the forbidden spiritual realm. This, the Bible predicts, will be prevalent in "the latter days" (1 Timothy 4:1).

Nostradamus's Curse Upon Unbelievers

Evidently, the issue as to the source of his prophecies was not up for discussion with Nostradamus. As far as he was concerned, all skeptics were infidels and he placed a damning curse on those who dared question his authority:

The Secrets of Nostradamus Exposed

*Those who read these verses, let them consider with
mature mind,
Let not the profane, vulgar and ignorant be attracted
to their study.
All Astrologers, Fools and Barbarians draw not near,
He who acts otherwise, is cursed according to rite.*

(Preface to Century 7).

As much as many would like to discard the term
"occult," and label the origin of Nostradamus's
prophecies with something more respectable, one
cannot deny that they were occultic in origin. But
what the prophet did is very common even today.
Destruction of nations doesn't always come in the
name of atheism. It usually comes through idolatry,
where leaders carry out their agenda, but with the
thought that "God is with us." It is a wrong concep-
tion of the nature of God which allows people to
create their own moral ethic.

Man has always been predisposed to idolatry.
Sometimes a god is shaped with the hands in wood
or stone form, sometimes it is shaped in the imagination, the place of imagery. When a man has his
own *image* of God, that notion doesn't protest even
when demons manifest in its name--because the
reality of the image is non-existent. Think of how
many people commit grisly crimes and say that God

was their inspiration, or of all the wars that have been started in the name of God.

Of course Nostradamus didn't kill in the name of God, but he did claim that the Creator was his source of his occultic practices. This is in direct contradiction to what the Bible reveals of the character of God.

If the prophet was inspired by the Creator, then the Bible is fallacious and totally unreliable, because the God of the Bible forbad the very practices Nostradamus said He inspired. It is similar to a thief saying that God inspired him to steal, when the 8th Commandment states an unconditional, "Thou shalt not steal."

Either the thief is a liar, he is totally deceived, or the Bible is morally wrong to forbid theft.

The Mantle of Bright Light

In a preface to *Nostradamus, Countdown To Apocalypse* by Jean-Charles de Fontbrune, (Henry Hold and Company), Elizabeth Greene speaks about his prophetic incantations:

"The practice of mouthing incantations, drawing pentagrams on the floor of one's study...and sliding into a trance in which the processes of history are revealed through strange shapes and visions would earn the practitioner an entry ticket to institutions like Bellevue or the Maudsley clinic rather than claim to undying fame and the favor of kings."

Her words were written back in 1983. It's a pity she didn't have a glimpse into the future and see that such practices would become the hobby of celebrities, the custom of President's wives and the methods of the CIA, rather than put one in a mental institution.

What she says next is the mentality that no doubt opened the door of respectability for the occult:

"Instead of that annoying word 'trance' we have a modern term, *abaissement du niveau mental*, coined in the early days of psychology to describe the lowering of the threshold of consciousness that occurs naturally in sleep and fantasy, and unnaturally in delirium, drugged states and psychosis. For Nostradamus this meant opening himself to visions from God about the future. For the modern explorer of the human psyche it means opening oneself to the archetypal images in the depths of the unconscious. Of those depths we know perilously little, save that, in the light of research by such giants as

Jung*, the unconscious can indeed be prophetic, not only in personal terms but in universal ones as well."

The apparition which manifest for King Saul was covered with a mantle, so that its face was not clearly seen. So is the face of the occult. Its appearance is as a mantle of bright light, but it is in truth the gross darkness of the spirit kingdom. While most psychics claim that God is the source of their light, their god certainly isn't the God revealed in Holy Scripture as the Creator of all things.

There is however, another god of which the Bible speaks. He is called "the god of this world" 2 Corinthians 4:4). The Bible tells us that he can (transform himself in to "an angel of light" (2 Corinthians 11:4).

That means that Satan is able to *disguise* himself as a *messenger* of light.

* Carl Gustav Jung was one of the original students of Freud who became a leading psychologist of the 20th Century.

Chapter Three
Famous Prophecies of a Famous Prophet

Nostradamus is a household name. He was the subject of a major Hollywood motion picture. Thousands of books have been written about him and his incredible predictions. Tabloids quote him. Video stores carry documentaries on his work. His life and prophecies have appeared with the famous on cable A & E's "Biography." This is why:

"With the passing of time, we have come to realize that Nostradamus accurately forecast a host of happenings, ranging from an English naval blitz on Spanish treasure ships at Cadiz to Adolf Hitler's machinations of war; from the invention of the submarine, airplane and Montgolfier balloon to the era of space stations and nuclear war." (*Predictions*, Fisher and Commins).

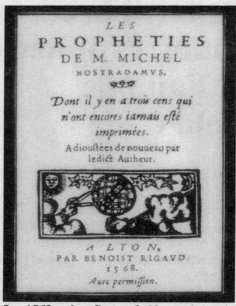

In 1568, the first of Nostradamus's complete prophecies was published posthumously in France.

Add to this the invention of the radio, the light bulb, the great fire of London, the Kennedy assassination, man landing on the moon and even the naming of America in prophecy, and we can see why he is so highly acclaimed.

Let's now look at some of the applauded prophecies of Michel de Nostredame and their incredible interpretations from French into English:

1. The invention of the radio and the light bulb:

When the animal is tamed by man
After great efforts and difficulty begins to speak,
The lightning so harmful to the rod
Will be taken from the earth and suspended in the air. (C3 Q44)

The *animal* in this quatrain which is tamed by man *after great efforts and difficulty begins to speak*, is the radio (*Nostradamus and the Millennium*, John Hogue (page 80). The *lightning* is the light bulb.

Experts tell us the prophet saw visions of the light bulb and other inventions with such clear illumination, he was more than likely tempted to bring them back from the future into his own time. We are told that he must have been bewildered as he tried to put into his own words what he was seeing in the hereafter, 300 years before that which he was seeing would come to pass.

2. America actually named in prophecy:

The rule is left to two, they will hold it for a very short time,
After three years and seven months they will go to war.
Their vessels rebel against them
The victor born on American soil. (C4 Q95)

Did the prophecies of Nostradamus mention the United States of America?

The Secrets of Nostradamus Exposed

This is taken *word for word* from, *Nostradamus and the Millennium* (page 149). Incredibly, America is actually *identified* in this prediction by the great prophet (in the fourth line). This is clearly the revolutionary war against England. Ships are referred to and there is even an allusion as to who would win the war.

However, there is a small quandary with the quatrain. Here is the same *word for word* quatrain taken from, *The Complete Prophecies of Nostradamus* (page 142):

The reign left to two they shall not keep it long,
Three years and seven months being past,
The vestals shall rebel against them,
The youngest shall be the conqueror of the Armorick country. (C4 Q95)

Let's see if the author picks up that what has become "the Armorick country" in the fourth line is actually Nostradamus speaking of the United States of America:

"This signifies a Kingdom that shall be left to two, who shall keep it but a short while. Their title will be challenged by two Nuns."

Here is the same quatrain from Edgar Leoni's, *Nostradamus and His Prophecies*:

The realm left to two they will hold it very briefly,
Three years and seven months passed by they will make war:
The two vestals will rebel in opposition,
Victor the younger in the land of Brittany. (C4 Q95)

Let's see if Edgar sees that what has now become the "land of Brittany" is the United States of America:

"...or 'Armenia.' Rather doubtful, unless the quatrain concerns Turkish or Persian princes." (page 249)

The celebrated English medium, Doris Collins maintained that she once made contact with the dead Nostradamus, and the subject came up about his Catholic faith. He told her (probably in English):

"I was born a Jew and although I changed my religion, it did not alter the fact that I was born a Jew."

It's a shame she didn't ask him what he was talking about in this quatrain.

3. The naming of Adolf Hitler.

Adolf Hitler was born in Austria, and earned a scanty living during his youth as an artist in Vienna. He joined the German army at the outbreak of World War One and served as a corporal in the trenches. When Germany surrendered in 1918, this stirred him enough to become involved in the political arena. He took over a small extremist party called the National Socialist German Worker's party, or the "Nazis." He failed in an attempt to seize power in 1923, was arrested and placed in prison for five years. This was where he wrote his political philosophy, *Mein Kampf* (My Struggle).

Hitler held extreme national and racist convictions, with a blazing hatred for the Jews. But after the German economy collapsed in 1929, many German people began to vote for him. In 1932, the Nazis became Germany's largest political party. The following year, Hitler was appointed as the chancellor of Germany, soon eliminated all opposition and established himself as the Fuhrer.

In 1939, after having rebuilt the German military, he invaded Poland and launched his country into World War Two. During the war, he began his "final solution"--the attempted extermination of the Jewish people. He managed to murder six million.

After two years of war, he was the conqueror of most of Europe, but this was short-lived. By 1945, allied forces had defeated his armies. On April 30, 1945, he apparently committed suicide in his bunker in Berlin and the last of the German forces surrendered on May 8 of the same year.

Experts have told us for years that Nostradamus

© Softkey Int'l

Did Nostradamus actually name Hitler in prophecy?

actually named this German dictator in his prophecies. Let's have a close look at what they say (these quatrains are taken directly from, *The Complete*

46

Prophecies of Nostradamus, Henry C. Roberts--
Occult Edition: "The only unabridged, definitive
edition of the authentic words of Nostradamus since
1672"):

In the year that is to come soon, and not far from
Venus,
The two greatest ones of Asia and Africa,
Shall be said to come from the Rhine and Ister,
Crying and tears shall be at Malta and on the
Italian Shore. (C4 Q68)

This is the foundation upon which the "Hitler"
interpretation is built. If you weren't perceptive
enough to find it for yourself, Hitler's name is the
last word on the third line of the quatrain: *Ister*.

We now look at the same quatrain, this time
from, *Nostradamus and His Prophecies* (Occult
sciences), by Edgar Leoni, 1982, Bell Publishing
Company, New York:

In the place very near not far from Venus,
The two greatest ones of Asia and of Africa,
From the Rhine and Lower Danube they will be said
to have come,

Cries, tears at Malta and Ligurian side. (C4 Q68)

Hitler has now become "the Lower Danube." But there is more evidence in other quatrains that this is indeed Hitler to whom the prophet is referring:

The great one of Mayence to quench a great thirst,
Shall be deprived of his high dignity,
Those of Cologne shall mourn him so much
That the Great Groppe shall be thrown into the Rhine. (C6 Q40)

There is the Fuhrer once again. He is here cited as the *Great Groppe.* If you are not a believer yet, there is further confirmation. This time it is an actual prediction that mentions Hitler and Mussolini, as well as Mussolini's flight to Germany after losing his power, then the eventual ruin of both of the dictators:

The year following being discovered by a flood,
Two chiefs elected, the first shall not hold,
To fly from shade, to one shall be a refuge
That house shall be plundered which shall maintain the first. (C9 Q4)

Finally, we see the death of Hitler, found here among the more than the one thousand prophecies of Nostradamus:

He who by iron shall destroy his father, born in Nonnaire,
Shall in the end carry the blood of the gorgon,
Shall in a strange country make all so silent,
That he shall burn himself, and his double talk.
(C8 Q79)

It seems that the truth has been stretched just a little for some reason. Others have also noticed this inconsistency:

"Some of these interpretations seem to involve a wilful ignorance of historical fact. For instance, verses referring to "Hister" have been translated by some commentators as referring to Hitler; however Hister was simply the Latin name that Nostradamus used for the river Danube. Indeed in one quatrain, the seer refers to the completion of a bridge across the Hister." *Visions & Prophecies*, page 20 (Timelife Books)

So if it is the Fuhrer, it seems that a bridge was

constructed across his back.

4. The dropping of the atomic bomb:

On August 6, 1945, the United States dropped the first atomic bomb on the Japanese city of Hiroshima. As the bomb detonated, a white cloud like an enormous mushroom, rose 50,000 feet into the sky. There was a blinding burst of light throughout the city. All that remained of Hiroshima was ruins and ashes. More than 80,000 people were

© Softkey Int'l

Did Nostradamus predict the mushroom cloud of the atomic bomb dropped on Japan in August of 1945?

killed in the immediate blast.

Many believe that Nostradamus is pointing to this event in the following prophecy:

Near the harbors within two cities,
There will happen two scourges the like of which was never before seen,
Famine, pestilence within, people put out by the sword.
Then cry for help from the great immortal God!

(C2 Q6)

Expert John Hogue explains:

"The words of this quatrain, numbered six, possibly after August 6, 1945, the day Hiroshima was irradiated, capture the prophet's horror while witnessing the two Japanese ports sacrificed on the altar of the dawning Nuclear Age." (*page 89, Nostradamus and the Millennium*).

However, Jean-Charles de Fontbrune, the author of the "sensational sequel to the best-selling and definitive *Nostradamus:Countdown to Apocalypse*" interprets the same prophecy (C2 Q6) a little differently:

"Clearly predicts the Berlin Wall which divides the city in two. *Two cities near the gate.*" (Brandenberg)

5. The prediction of the French President Charles De Gaulle (1958-1970):

In his book, *Nostradamus and the Millennium*, John Hogue directly quotes C9 Q33 (page 93), where the prophet actually *mentions* de Gaulle by name:

"...for three times one surnamed de Gaulle will lead France..." (line 2 of the quatrain).

Here now is the same C9 Q33 from, *The Complete Prophecies of Nostradamus*, by Henry C. Roberts--reprinted in 1982 (page 289):

Hercules, King of Rome, and Denmark,
Of France three Guyon surnamed,
Shall cause Italy to quake and one of Venice,
He shall be above all a famous monarch. (C9 Q33)

President de Gaulle has now become "three Guyon." Here now is Henry C. Robert's (de Gaulle-less) interpretation of the prophecy:

"We believe that the 'Hercules' referred to indicates the powerful and famous Napoleon, before whom all Europe quaked." President de Gaulle is actually Napoleon.

But Edgar Leoni in his publication, *Nostradamus and His Prophecies* translates the same quatrain:

Hercules King of Rome and of "Annemark,"
With the surname of the chief of triple Gaul,
Italy and the one of St. Mark to tremble,
First monarch renowned above all. (C9 Q33)

His commentary on "Gaul" is:

"...i.e., the surname of the one-time (58-49 B.C.) ruler of Gaul, Caesar or Imperator, title borne by the (Holy) Roman Emperor." (page 391)

Take your pick: de Gaulle, Napoleon or Caesar.

6. The landing of man on the moon:
He shall come to the corner of Luna,
Where he shall be taken and put in a strange land,
The green fruits shall be in great disorder,
A great shame, to one shall be great praise.

(C9 Q65)

Here is what has been called by some, a "remarkable forecast" of man landing on the moon. However, Edgar Leoni, the author of, *Nostradamus and His Prophecies* comments on *Luna*:

"The possibilities here are numerous. Possibly Lunigiana."

© Softkey Int'l

Man on the moon--did the 16th Century French prophet see this event?

7. The assassination of President Kennedy and Senator Robert Kennedy:

In 1960, at the age of just 43 years, John F. Kennedy became President of the United States. He was the youngest man ever elected to the office of

President. He was born in Brookline, Massachusetts, and served in the United States navy in World War Two, narrowly escaping death when the boat he commanded was fired on and sunk by a Japanese destroyer. He served as a democratic representative for Massachusetts, and was later elected to the Senate.

While functioning as president, he showed great fortitude during the difficult "Cuban Missile Crisis" of 1962. In 1963, he signed a nuclear treaty with the Soviet Union, and in November of the same year, he was tragically assassinated in Dallas, Texas.

Experts maintain that the following quatrain is a very clear prediction of President Kennedy and his brother's murder:

The great man will be struck down in the day by a thunderbolt,
The evil deed predicted by the bearer of a petition:
According to the prediction another falls at night time.
Conflict in Reims, London, and pestilence in Tuscany.

(C1 Q26)

President John Fitzgerald Kennedy was shot and killed shortly after twelve noon in Dallas, Texas, on

November 22, 1963. His brother was killed a few minutes after one in the morning in California. It is said that Jean Dixon, one of the foremost psychics of modern times predicted his assassination as early as

© Softkey Int'l

Was Nostradamus able to see the assassination of President Kennedy and his brother?

August 1952, 11 years earlier. She maintains that she was kneeling before a statue of the virgin Mary when the vision came to her.

The experts who believe that this prophecy is in reference to the Kennedy brothers also believe that Nostradamus indicated that the third brother, Edward Kennedy, would become President of the United States.

That's one interpretation. Here's another exegesis of the same quatrain from another eminent expert, who says it was:

"The taking over of Czechoslovakia by Hitler, the resignation of President Benes, the dissensions over the matter between France and England and the dire warning of the consequences of this betrayal, are all remarkably outlined in this prophecy" (Henry C. Roberts, page 17, *The Complete Prophecies of Nostradamus*)

8. The space shuttle tragedy:

Nine will be set apart from the human flock
Separated from judgement and counsel:
Their fate to be determined on departure...
...The unripe fruit will be the source of great scandal

The Secrets of Nostradamus Exposed

Great blame, to the other great praise.

(C1 Q81)

Few can forget the horror of the space shuttle tragedy. Here is the interpretation by John Hogue, the author of *Nostradamus and the Millennium* (he makes quick reference to the fact that there were seven astronauts in the Challenger tragedy, not nine as stated by Nostradamus):

"Except for the mistake in numbers, Nostradamus

Did Nostradamus see the Challenger explode and take the lives of seven Americans?

comes amazingly close in describing the greatest space tragedy to date. On January 28th, 1986, seventy-one seconds after liftoff, seven astronauts of the spaceship Challenger were killed when volatile gases leaking from the left solid rocket-booster enveloped them in a tremendous explosion.

"NASA--the US space agency--endured its own Watergate during the following months of investigation which brought to the world's attention flaws in design and command decisions leading to the launching of Challenger.

"The US space effort was scandalized for sending their astronauts on the *unripe fruit* of faulty rocket-boosters in an effort to cut the budget.

"During the same period the Soviet Space program continued to run smoothly with the complete support of its government and people *to the other great praise.*"

Here now is the exact same prophecy from the pen of Henry C. Roberts (*The Complete Prophecies of Nostradamus*):

Of the human flock, nine shall be set aside,
Being divided in judgment and counsel,
Their destiny shall be to be divided,

The Secrets of Nostradamus Exposed

Kappa, Theta, Lambda, dead, banished, scattered.
                                        (C1 Q81)

Here is his interpretation:

"The Supreme Court of the United States, consisting of nine members is here indicated, as well as the Ploituro of the U.S.S.R. More than once has death and dismissal involved both bodies." (page 36)

9. Try your own interpretation:

A treasure put in a temple by Hesperian citizens,
In the same hid in a secret place,
The hungry serfs shall cause the temple to open,
And take again and ravish, a fearful prey in
the middle.

The explanation:

"The treasure (gold) placed in the temple (Fort Knox) by Hesperian (Western) citizens. Economic chaos and uprisings shall cause an attempt to storm Fort Knox." (Henry C. Roberts)

In this prophecy Nostradamus is looking far ahead in time and seeing a robbery of Fort Knox take place.

The Secrets of Nostradamus Exposed

Throw enough black paint on a white wall, and the simple will see the face of Jesus, and light candles in homage.

The *interpretations* of the prophecies of Nostradamus are fantastic in the truest sense of the word. But despite the imaginations of overzealous interpreters, there are some fascinating prophecies which came from the pen of the French prophet. He predicted submarines, fighter pilots and he even foretold a time when people will travel safely by air:

Pestilence extinguished, the world becomes small
For a long time the lands will be inhabited in peace.
People will travel safely by air, land, seas and wave.
Then wars will start again. (C1 Q63)

How did he get these incredible insights? This we will look into in the next chapter.

Chapter Four
Amazing Prophecies

Nostradamus warned that the future would bring signs in the sun. Interestingly enough, so does the Bible. He forewarned of earthquakes. So does the Bible. He spoke of the earth being round. So does the Bible. He warned of a coming world leader--the anti-Christ. So does the Bible. He speaks of the dead coming out of their graves. So does the Bible. He prophesied that the Jews would get Israel back. So does the Bible. He said that the Middle East would play a central role in the last days. So does the Bible. He said there would be signs in the sky. So does the Bible. He forecast the binding of Satan. So does the Bible. He spoke of great famines and the cost of a bushel of wheat. So does the Bible. He spoke of Satan being bound for one thousand years.

So does the Bible. He didn't however, talk about false prophets and their direct relationship to deceitful demonic spirits. The Bible does:

"Beloved, do not believe every spirit, but test the spirits, whether they are of God; *because many false prophets have gone out into the world*" (1 John 4:1, italics added).

Look at these almost biblically accurate predictions of Nostradamus taken from, *Nostradamus into the Twenty-first Century,* Jean-Charles de Fontbrune (published in 1985)--the author's words are in italics:

"...The people will rise up to resist and attack those who would promulgate new laws; also it seems that the countries weakened by the Orientals (*USSR, Poland, Rumania, Czechoslovakia, Hungary, East Germany and Bulgaria*) may be victims of Satan freed by the creator of infernal prisons, in order to bring to birth great Gog and Magog who shall wreak so much abominable destruction upon the Churches that the reds (*Communists*) and the whites (*Moslems*) shall thereby lose their judgment, power and strength...but their (*Soviet*) fleet will be weakened by the Westerners, and this country (*USSR*) will know a great desolation; her greatest cities shall be depopulated and those who enter therein shall serve the vengeance of the wrath of God."

Then Jean-Charles de Fontbrune says: *"This section from the Letter to Henri should be compared with Ezekiel 38"*:

"Son of man, set thy face against Gog, the land of Magog, the chief prince of Meshech (*Moscow*) and Tubal (*Tobolsk*) and prophesy against him...And I will turn thee back, and put hooks into thy jaws, and I will bring thee forth, and all thine army, horses and horsemen, all of them clothed with all sorts of armor (*tank divisions*)....Persia (*Iran*), Ethiopia, and Libya with them; all of them with shield and helmet (*Russian armaments*)...Gomer (*Turkey*), and all his bands; the house of Togarmah-...and many people with thee...in the latter years (*before 1999*) thou shalt come into the land that is brought back from the sword, and is gathered out of many people (*the State of Israel in 1948*), against the mountains of Israel..."

Then, with widened eyes and mouth, the French author says:

"There is a remarkable parallel between Nostradamus and these two chapters of Ezekiel..."

I wonder why...

His "Divine" Source

The divinations of Nostradamus contain words and phrases such as "milk and honey," "tribulation," "anti-Christ," "pestilence," "latter" days, "God loosed Satan," "seventy times," "Gog and Magog," "trodden down," "fire and sword," "the sea shall be red," "great tribulation as ever did happen," etc. These are *biblically*-based expressions, betraying why many of his prophecies seem to have come to pass.

It is clear that Nostradamus was familiar with the Bible as he often quotes from or refers to its passages. A 1981 Warner Brothers documentary about the life of Nostradamus confirms this fact:

"His ancestors where Jewish--his family had converted to Christianity. So when his grandfather adopted him, he studied the Cabbalah (an occult system originating in a mystical interpretation of the Scriptures among certain Jewish rabbis) as well as the Old and the New Testaments."

Why are so many of his prophecies so accurate? *Because he merely hung his own clothes on the body of Holy Scripture, and when the body came alive, he claimed to be the Creator.*

I am sure that Russia will attack Israel. If I publicly state that fact without making it clear that the fountain of my belief is the Bible, when Russia attacks Israel, I too may be heralded in the future as a great prophet by those who are ignorant of biblical content.

Nostradamus didn't have extra sensory perception, nor was he inspired by the flame of the Holy Spirit. He was educated and secretly read the Holy Scriptures, something forbidden by the Roman Catholic church of his day. The church was already plagued with what it saw as the curse of Protestants, who were Protestants because they read that Book.

Take for example the words of Jean-Charles de Fontbrune, as he expounds on how he thought Nostradamus "enriched" his prophecies, in a chapter called *On Method* in his book, *Nostradamus, Countdown To Apocalypse*, (page xxxv):

"I could imagine Nostradamus in his study consulting many erudite literary, historical and geographical works to codify the vision which had been vouchsafed him. I became even more convinced of this when I was confronted with the huge mass of documentation and the cross-reference which I myself needed, first to understand the meaning of quatrains, then to collate them with the historical events they were describing."

The author admits that many do believe that Nostradamus, in his letter to his son Cesar, discloses his practice of plagiarism (literary theft):

"Many have speculated about the following passage from the Letter to his son Cesar: 'Fearing lest various books which have been hidden for centuries be discovered, and dreading what might happen to them, I presented them to Vulcan.' This has been taken to mean that *Nostradamus had a secret library upon which he drew for his prophecies, taking all the credit without acknowledging his debt...*" (page xxxiv, italics added)

Undoubtedly, within this secret library from which he drew his prophecies and took credit for them, was a well-used Bible which contained the sure to be fulfilled words of the prophets.

If Nostradamus combined his biblical knowledge of future events with one thousand other occult prophecies, there are bound to be a number which fit the bill. Discharge one thousand arrows into the air, and some are destined to hit a target--especially if God has already preordained that they hit their mark.

Nostradamus made prime time news with his predictions. Add to this the exaggerated hearsay of the verbal tabloids of his day, and you have a reputation, recognition and booming book sales. As time passes, you may even have people lining up to drink wine from your empty skull.

A Necessary Platform

Study closely the following captivating quatrain:

Fine line of soldiers fighting
War in the East without heat
Locusts and honey feast with no end
To the North rides the man of iron.

Here is the interpretation:

"In 1814, Napoleon sent lines of his finest troops into the east of Spain during winter. In the heat of the battle, a plague of locusts, attracted by the warm south winds descended upon the troops bringing confusion to the enemy. This enabled

Napoleon to lead his victorious company north-ward." *Powerful stuff*.

If you have half a mind to, you may believe that event happened. I doubt it. The "quatrain" came from my own ripe imagination. However, it would-n't surprise me that if you studied the millions of events of history, you would soon find some inter-esting happening to hang it on.

This thought is well summarized by Jean Gimon in a book published on the history of Salon in 1882:

"The style of the *Centuries* is so multiform and nebulous that each may, with a little effort and good will, find in them what he seeks. Like airy vapors, they assume, as they unroll, the figures of which the spectator's imagination lends them, and this fact assures this sibylline work of an immense and eternal success with those who are devotees of the marvelous." *Chroniques de Salon* (Aix, 1882)

The forecastings of Nostradamus are often so vague, they can be shaped by the hands of the wildest imagination. There are no bounds as to how far they may be stretched to fit. Look at this inter-esting stretch of the imagination from Elizabeth Greene in the preface of, *Nostradamus Countdown To Apocalypse*:

"To Nostradamus a king meant only one thing: the physical king of a physical country. We, however, are somewhat more sophisticated now. There are not many kings left these days, and though they rule, they do not govern as they once did. Now we have presidents and prime ministers, juntas and governing committees. More fancifully, perhaps, there are also inner rulers: dominant ideas, governing our morals and values, little petty tyrants of our minds and souls, benign spiritual leaders that we call our good will or our higher principles. What if an inner king, rather than an outer one, retrieved his lost throne at the end of the millennium? What if the great war that Nostradamus foresees were a psychological battlefield, rather than a physical one? Like an image from a dream, the Great King ruling by right of heaven is open to many levels of interpretation, and they all occur at once."

The phrase "we, however, are somewhat more sophisticated now," is more than just an inference that Nostradamus was a simpleton. It is her most necessary platform to explain how to make a prophecy about kings fit, when there is a shortage of kings upon which to fit them. If the handsome prince has to snap off a few toes to make the glass slipper fit, so be it.

Chapter Five
Goodbye New York

Shakespeare reminded us that the devil can quote scripture. He quoted the Bible to Jesus Christ. For thousands of years, the entity that scripture calls the "spirit that works in the children of disobedience," has seen Biblical prophecies come to pass. He knows the "signs of the times" better than the most avid of Bible scholars. In the case of Nostradamus, the "father of lies" deceived the simple by speaking some scriptural truths through a familiar spirit. It wasn't the first time he did it, and it won't be the last. However, in this case millions who are not familiar with those biblical truths, have been hoodwinked by a pied piper playing Someone else's tune.

If you are too scholarly to believe in the devil, then you are calling the God of the Bible, a liar. It is *His* Word that uncovers the spiritual source of all evil as being Satan. We are told that he came to "kill, steal and destroy," that he blinds the minds and deceives nations. The fact of your irrational denial of a source of evil, when evil is so incredibly conspicuous in this world, confirms what the Scriptures say of his labors. The Bible is a resumé of his corrupt persona. Here is a quick synopsis of his background, work and character:

He is called the father of lies (John 8:44).
He is the prince of this world (John 12:31).
He is also the god of this world (2 Cor. 4:4).
He tempts to disobedience (Genesis 3:4).
He is a slanderer (Job 1:9).
He inflicts disease (Job 2:7, Luke 13:16).
He hides the truth of the Gospel (Matthew 13:19).
He inspires hypocrisy (Matthew 13:38).
He ruins the body and soul (Luke 9:42).
He induces lies and murder (John 8:44).
He is our spiritual father (John 8:44).
He inspired Judas to betrayal (John 13:2).
He is like a roaring, devouring lion (1 Peter 5:8).
He is the prince of demons (Matthew 9:34).
He deceives the nations through sorceries (Revelation 18:23).
He has the power to blind the mind and keep it in darkness (Acts 26:18, 2 Corinthians 4:4).

He governs over the "principalities, powers, rulers of the darkness of this world" (Eph. 6:12).
He has all power, with "lying signs and wonders" (2 Thessalonians 2:9).

If you study Church history, you will see that Satan persecuted the true Church down through the ages--especially through the "Mother of Harlots," who sat on seven mountains (Revelation 17:1-9--Greek *oros* meaning a "hill" or "mount"). She is also referred to as the "great city" (Revelation 17:18), and the Bible says she was drunk with the spilled blood of those who trusted in Jesus Christ (Revelation 18:24, 19:1-2).

The devil even tempted Jesus to enter the occult realm by becoming a satan-worshipper (Matthew 4:9).

The Bible has much to say about the devil. The Greek word for *devil* is "diablos," which means "adversary, false accuser or slanderer." The word is used 34 times in scripture. In another 76 places the word *devil* and *devils* are found. These are references to evil spirits or demons. There is only one prince of demons, but there are many demons. Demons are spirits, which don't seem to be able to materialize unless they operate through the possession of humans or animals (Revelation 16:13-16, see Matthew 8:30-32).

Here are some of the characteristics and work of demons:

They are intrinsically evil (Judges 9:23).
They are shrewd (Acts 16:16).
They are powerful (Mark 5:1-18).
They possess human beings (Mark 1:32).
They have miraculous powers (Revelation 16:14).
They can be exorcised from humans (Matt. 10:7-8).

When someone ignores his conscience and calls upon demons for "guidance," the demons will gladly oblige. All that is necessary for demonic possession is a seeking heart and an empty mind.

Demonic Deceit

Author Edgar Leoni said of Nostradamus:

"The two principal foundation stones for his prophecies are magic and astrology. From the evidence we have, it would seem that when the spirit moved him, Nostradamus would go up to his secret study, lock himself in, get out his magic paraphernalia including a brass bowl, tripod and laurel branch, and proceed to go through the demon-evoking formulas prescribed by Jamblichus." *Nostradamus and His Prophecies*, (Bell Publishing Company, page 108)

Nostradamus was deceived because he practiced that which his own heart warned him against. Why would he *fear* if he knew he was doing what was right? He emptied his soul, brain and heart, and that method was believed to help Nostradamus "overcome a strong barrier of fear which came upon him before he surrendered his will in the occultic trance." He embraced that which the Bible says is an "abomination" to the Lord:

"There shall not be found among you...a soothsayer, or one who interprets omens, or a sorcerer, or one who conjures spells, or a medium, or a spiritist, or one who calls up the dead. For all these things are an abomination to the Lord..." (Deuteronomy 18:10-12).

Nostradamus didn't always use his standard procedure. Now and then he did work with "omens." An omen is a "phenomenon or incident regarded as a prophetic sign." Edgar Leoni expounds this practice:

"Omens to the right and left served to make him

77

more sure of his convictions. One such omen is mentioned by Cesar (*Histoire de Provence*, page 775):

The year 1554...I don't know what sad and unhappy events begin and follow creatures hideously deformed and prodigious. Scarcely had January expired when one saw born at Senas a monstrous child, having two heads, which the eye could not look at without some sort of horror: he had been predicted some time previously by those who had knowledge of the course of future events...He was carried to my father and seen by several persons.

"This, and the birth of a two-headed horse near Salon forty-five days later, caused Nostradamus to declare profoundly that a deep cleavage in France was ahead." (*Nostradamus and His Prophecies*, Edgar Leoni, page 25)

This is one way he found out what was ahead. Did he really conclude that this two-headed child was a sign from God? Why didn't He speak to him through a spirit rather than give some poor child a second head just to show Nostradamus a sign of a future event? Does God do such things? I don't think so. The Bible tells us how God speaks:

"God, who at various times and in different ways spoke in time past to the fathers by the prophets, has in these last days spoken to us by His Son, whom He has appointed heir of all things, through Whom He also made the worlds" (Hebrews 1:1-2).

Since the Day of Pentecost we have the Holy Spirit--the "Spirit of Truth," who "leads into all truth." The Word of God is a "lamp to my feet and a light to my path." The Holy Spirit makes the Word of God come alive (2 Corinthians 3:6). Look now of Whom the Holy Spirit testifies:

"But when the Comforter is come, whom I will send unto you from the Father, even the Spirit of Truth, which proceedeth from the Father, *He shall testify of Me*" (John 15:26, italics added).

Look at what Jesus further said of the Holy Spirit and prophecy:

"However, when He, the Spirit of Truth, has come, He will guide you into all truth; for He will not speak on His own authority, but whatever He hears He will speak; and He will tell you of things to come. *He will glorify Me*, for He will take of Mine and declare it to you" (John 16:13-14, italics added).

If the Holy Spirit was, as Nostradamus claims, testifying through him, why didn't He attest even once to the deity of Jesus Christ? The Apostles did continually. They preached the person of Jesus Christ. In fact the New Testament mentions the name *Jesus* and the title *Christ* an incredible 1528 times! The Apostle Paul in one of his epistles refers to Jesus Christ by name no less that ten times in eight short verses. The Savior is the life's blood of those who are possessed by the Holy Spirit. He is "the Alpha and the Omega, the Beginning and the End, the First and the Last" (Revelation 22:13). You cannot separate the testimony of Jesus Christ from the spirit of prophecy, for "the testimony of Jesus *is* the spirit of prophecy" (Revelation 19:10, italics added).

When John, by the Holy Spirit's inspiration wrote the Book of Revelation he wrapped it in the person of Jesus Christ. It begins with, "The Revelation of Jesus Christ." The second verse says, "Who bore witness...to the testimony of Jesus Christ." The book concludes with, "Amen. Even so, come Lord Jesus! The grace of our Lord Jesus Christ be with you. Amen."

Why would the Holy Spirit exalt Jesus? The answer is in the Book of Philippians:

"...Christ Jesus, who, being in the form of God, did not consider it robbery to be equal with God, but made himself of no reputation, taking the form of a servant, and coming in the likeness of men. And being found in appearance as a man, He humbled Himself and became obedient to the point of death, even the death of the cross. Therefore God also has highly exalted Him and given Him the name which is above every name, that at the name of Jesus every knee should bow, of those in heaven, and of those on earth and of those under the earth, and that every tongue should confess that Jesus Christ is Lord, to the glory of God the Father" (Philippians 2:5-11).

Nostradamus speaks many times about the Pope, the church, Israel, faith, the Scriptures and prayer. In his epistles, his letters and his prophecies, he talks of the Holy Spirit, of God and of Satan, but there is a conspicuous absence of any reference to the individual of Jesus Christ. There are a few exceptions where he uses His name to describe the Roman Catholic church, or as a fixed reference point in history.

He does however use the *words* of Jesus to justify not giving his occult utterances to those who appose his practices--"give not that which is holy to the dogs," saying that God has "hidden these things from the wise and prudent and revealed them unto babes." (*Preface by M. Nostradamus to His Prophecies*--Ibid, page xx)

The "Holy" Prophecies

Nostradamus wasn't the only one who considered his utterances to be holy. Elizabeth Greene begins a preface to a book about the prophet, comparing his words to those of Holy Scripture:

"The prophecies of Nostradamus are as indestructible as the Revelation of St. John..."

Look at the esteem given to Nostradamus by Jean-Charles de Fontbrune:

"However, we must not despair. If we had only the analyses of the politicians, doomswatchers, demographers, sociologists and economists to go by, man's horizon would be completely blocked. Absolute and irreversible pessimism would be the rule. The only remaining hope is the prophetic message brought to man. Whether the prophets are those of the Old or the New Testaments, Christ or Nostradamus, they all announce the realization of the 'Kingdom' when universal peace shall at last reign among men." (Epilogue, *Nostradamus Countdown to Apocalypse* (page 440)

Author, Francis X. King goes further than equating the prophecies of the seer with those of Jesus. In his book, which speaks much about the church, the Scriptures, the Kingdom, God, etc., there is again a conspicuous absence of reference to Jesus Christ. He does however make mention of Him on the last page, and in doing so reveals his profound ignorance of the Bible:

"On the other hand, in line with the theory of alterative realities, even Christ's prophecies seemed to have failed on occasion. He correctly predicted the fall of the Temple of Jerusalem in AD 70, when the Romans sacked it. However, he (*the author uses lower case*) also predicted incorrectly that the end of the world would come shortly after the destruction of the Temple." (*Nostradamus*, Francis X. King, page 169, St. Martin's Press)

Signs and Lying Wonders

Whether in ignorance or with intention, if we

mix the occult with the truths of the Bible, we *will* be greatly deceived. The following verses say why:

"The coming of the lawless one is according to the working of Satan, with all power, signs, and lying wonders, and with all unrighteous deception among those who perish, because they did not receive the love of the truth, that they might be saved. And for this reason *God will send them strong delusion, that they should believe the lie*, that they all may be condemned who did not believe the truth but had pleasure in unrighteousness" (2 Thessalonians 2:9-12, italics added).

If we prefer the darkness of the occult, rather than the light of God's Word, God Himself may give us over to that which we want. Look at the categories of those who are thrust outside of the Kingdom of God (dogs are here used metaphorically "of those whose moral impurity will exclude them from the New Jerusalem," *Vines Expository Dictionary of New Testament Words*, MacDonald):

"Blessed are those who do His commandments, that they may have the right to the tree of life, and may enter through the gates into the city. But outside are dogs and sorcerers and sexually immoral and murderers..." (Revelation 22:13-14).

Did drunken soldiers really drink wine from the skull of the dead prophet? We will find out in the next chapter.

Chapter Six
Increase in Prophets

In 1534, Nostradamus fled from the wrath of the Catholic church to Italy, during which time his prophetic powers began to become apparent. The story is told of him falling on his knees before a young Franciscan monk named Felix Peretti and addressing him as "Your Holiness." This prompted mockery from those who witnessed the event. They were aware that this man was not holy at all. He was just a former pig farmer from a humble background.

However, in time this lowly monk became Cardinal of Montalto and in 1585--nineteen years after the death of Nostradamus, he was proclaimed Pope Sixtis the Fifth.

The story is also told that while the budding

prophet was lodging at the castle of the Lord of Florinville, a skeptic decided he would test his prophetic powers. While they were strolling one day, the nobleman asked Nostradamus to predict the fate of two barnyard pigs, one white and one black. Nostradamus replied that the man would eat the black one and that the white pig would be devoured by a wolf. Secretly, the man had his cook kill the white pig and serve it for supper.

After the meal, the nobleman revealed what he had done, but the prophet so insisted that he was correct, that they called for the cook. It was then that they found what had happened. The cook had obeyed his master and killed and prepared the white pig. But as it sat ready for the oven, a wolf snuck into the kitchen and began eating the pig. Fearing the wrath of his master, the cook killed and prepared the black pig and served it. Thus the validity of the prediction was proven, and his reputation grew.

Another story is told of Nostradamus suffering an attack of gout. He was confined for ten days and was wanting to be alone. Suddenly, there began a persistent knocking at his door. It was a page of the illustrious family of Beauveau, who had lost a fine dog which had been entrusted to him.

Before the page could say why he was even

knocking on the door, Nostradamus called out, "What's the matter, king's page? You are making a lot of noise over a lost dog. Go and look on the road to Orleans. You will find it there, led on a leash." When the page was turned, he found a servant leading the dog back.

How much faith can you have in the stories of the pig-keeping monk, the wolf and the two little pigs, and the short tale of the lost dog? As much as you want. There is also nothing to stop you digging deep into your pocket at the check-out stand. If a paper claims: *Wife's Varicose Veins Form Map Leading To Hidden Treasure* or *Prophet Predicts Prepared Pork--Poor Pig Pilfered By Powerful Predator*, millions will no doubt open their mouths and their purses for more meaty details. To try and prove that the stories didn't happen is almost impossible.

There are many tales of "supernatural" happenings that cannot be scientifically substantiated (including those in the Bible). Take for example the three shepherd children near the Portuguese village of Fatima during the First World War. On May 13, 1917, three little girls (aged 7, 9, and 10 years old) told a story of seeing a "beautiful lady from Heaven" who talked to them for several minutes.

The vision promised to return, and we are told

it did so five more times, on the thirteenth of each of the following months. It wasn't long before 50,000 miracle seekers flocked to the "sacred" spot. Who was this lady? It was none other than the virgin Mary. As the crowd stood spell-bound, the virgin gave three messages of forthcoming events. *One problem.* Of the 50,000 who went there to witness the miracle, the only ones who saw Mary and heard her voice were the three girls.

The beautiful lady gave the children a message, that was to be written down and sealed, and not to be opened until the 1950s:

"It was later reported that Pope Pius XII had opened the message of Fatima: but no statement from the Vatican was forthcoming...unofficial sources rumored that the Pope had fainted when he read the contents of the letter..." (*Man, Myth & Magic*, Vol. 23, page 3131, Marshall Vavendish Corporation, New York)

Then there is the interesting story of the three inebriated soldiers who lifted Nostradamus's coffin out of the grave (recounted in the opening of the first chapter). They raised the lid to see a sight that paralyzed them--across the skeletal remains lay a plaque which read "May 1791." Nostradamus, who had been buried 200 years earlier, had incredibly predicted the *very date* of his exhumation.

Well, here is what apparently happened at his death:

"Having left us with this final vision of harmony, Nostradamus died in Salon in 1566 and was buried in the vault at the Church of St. Lawrence. His epitaph, translated from the original Latin reads:

Here rest the bones of the illustrious Michel Nostradamus, alone of all mortals judged worthy to record with his almost divine pen, under the influence of the stars, the future events of the entire world. He lived sixty-two years, six months and seventeen days." (*Predictions*, Fisher and Commins, van Nostrand Reinhold Company)

So the body of Nostradamus wasn't buried in a common grave, but was placed in a vault at the Church of St. Lawrence. *Don't be too sure*. If that did happened, then the executors of his will should have been incarcerated. The prophet's will states:

"Because after the soul the body is the most worthy thing at this time, the said testator has willed that when his soul has departed from his body, the latter will be carried to burial in the Church of the Covenant of St. Francis of the said Salon, and between its great door and the altar of St. Martha, where he has willed that his said body be accompanied by four candles, of one livre each, and he has willed also that all his obsequies and funeral rites be conducted at the discretion of his executors hereinafter named." (Last Will and Testament of Michel Nostradamus, *Nostradamus and His Prophecies*, Edgar Leoni, page 773)

We find out more information from Edgar Leoni in the biography section of the same book (page 37):

"His body was to be laid in the church of the Franciscan monastery between the great door and the altar of St. Martha. For this, the friars got one crown. The executors were to be Pallamedes Marc, Lord of Chateauneuf, and Jacques Suffren, bourgeois."

So it looks like those who put the body into the tomb at St. Francis were well paid for doing their job. Therefore, it seems that he wasn't exhumed. *Don't be too sure.*

Here are more details from the same publication:

"The soldiers of Revolutionary France seemed to have an insatiable craving for the violation of churches and tombs, and Nostradamus's tomb was no exception. In 1791, some Guardes Nationals from Marseilles broke into his tomb, quite heedless of the solemn warning. One of them is said to have drunk some wine out of the prophet's skull. The bones were scattered during this drunken orgy and the Salonians were only too glad of this opportunity to gather new relics. The Mayor, M. David, gathered together all the bones he could find, gaining the co-operation of the soldiery by ingeniously informing them that Nostradamus had predicted the Revolution. The remaining bones were placed in a wall of the Chapel of the Virgin in the Church of Saint-Laurent, Salon's other church, which escaped damage. In the interests of poetic justice, we are told that the 'sacrilegious' soldier was killed the next morning in an ambush near Lancon." (ibid, page 40)

So the soldier didn't die at the scene. Instead, he was killed the next morning in an ambush. *Don't be too sure*. The author then adds that another version is that he was caught with some stolen silverware and hanged. So it seems that there was no raising of the casket lid to see the plaque which read the exact

date of the exhumation. It also seems that there was
no dropping dead the instant the wine from the skull
touched the drunken soldier's lips.

Then again, we have a slightly different version
from some more experts:

"He died during the night of July 1 (1566), and was
buried upright in the wall of the Church of the
Cordeliers in Salon. In 1791 superstitious French
soldiers opened his grave. His bones were reburied
in the Church of St. Laurent, also in Salon."
*Harper's Encyclopedia of Mystical & Paranormal
Experiences*, Guiley, (Castle Books)

So it wasn't 200 years after his death, but 225
years. Then again, we can't be too sure of that.
According to, *They Foresaw the Future* (Glass,
G.P. Putman's Sons, New York), neither date is
correct. It seems that in on the night of July 1,
1566, after the bout with gout, Nostradamus made
his last prophecy. He said, "You will not see me
alive at sunrise." He was dead right. Let's see what
Mr. Glass says about what happened after the
prophet's death:

"Nearly fifty years after his death the authorities of
Salon decided to remove his coffin to a place of

greater importance in the church. In the hope that other predictions might have been buried with him, the casket was opened and there, on his breastbone, was a small metal plate, engraved with the date of the exhumation. He had foreseen even that."

So if we are seeing clearly through Glass, there was no threat of a curse, no drunken French soldiers, no drinking of wine from the skull, no shot from a stray bullet and it wasn't a period of 200 years until the supposed exhumation, but a mere 50 years.

However, that may not be true. The well-known psychic Mary Devlin first establishes that the prophecies of Nostradamus are "well documented" and have "proven accurate to degree far beyond the realm of chance." Then she says:

"Perhaps the most errie of his prophecies was the desecration of his own grave. When superstitious soldiers opened Nostradamus's coffin in May of 1789, around the corpse's neck was a medallion bearing the very date of his disinternment." *Horoscope*, (January 1996, page 48-49)

So, it was in 1789 that the desecration took place. That's 223 years after his death. Also, the medallion wasn't on his breastplate, but had been placed around his neck.

This now leaves us with three "well-document-ed" choices. He was either, 1. In a vault at the Church of St. Lawrence, 2. With the next door neighbor--St. Martha in the Church of the Covenant of St. Francis, or 3. Not in a coffin at all, but was sitting upright in the wall of the Church of Cordeliers.

Another expert sheds more light on the incident:

"...tales had begun to spread concerning manu-scripts or treasures allegedly interred within his tomb...So strong was the belief in these legends that in 1700 the grave was opened by a gang of daring tomb-robbers. The robbers found neither treasure nor documents containing hitherto unknown Nost-radamus revelations--but the tomb contained, as well as the bones of the seer, a thin, gilded medal-lion. On it were the letters MDCC--the Latin equivalent of 1700, the year in which the thieves committed their act of sacrilege." *Nostradamus*, Francis X. King, page 17, St. Martin's Press)

By now it should be clear what actually hap-pened--there is one more detail to add:

"On his deathbed he asked his wife to have his

body placed upright in the wall of Salon's Church of the Cordeliers. A rumor spread through the following centuries that a secret document existed inside his coffin that would decode all his prophecies. In 1700, the city fathers decided to move his illustrious corpse to a more prominent wall of the church. They took a quick look inside, careful not to disturb the body since they were aware of the quatrain warning against desecrating his grave. No paper was found, only a practical joke which had taken one hundred and thirty-four years for the punchline: on his skeleton hung a medallion with the year 1700 inscribed." *Nostradamus & the Millennium*, John Hogue, page 52-53 (Dolphin Books)

So the incident wasn't 50 years, not 200 years, not 215 years, not 223 years, not 125 years, but it happened 134 years after the prophet's death. It was actually *grave-robbers* (or city fathers) that opened the tomb not drunken soldiers. No promise of inheriting powers, no fearful curse, no wine drunk from the skull, no dropping dead, and no specific mentioning of the month of the exhumation.

Whatever happened, the story is typical of how reputations are made. Perhaps this tale made the prophet out to be a little more than he was.

Well, at least he was a great physician. At least he was a prominent healer "who would have stood out in history had he not made one prediction." Not according to one expert:

"He would seem to have been much more successful in treating victims of *le charbon* than most of his medical contemporaries. This was probably not because of any great virtue in the remedies he used in therapy, the formulae of some of which have survived. One of them, for instance, was compounded of rose petals, cloves, lignum aloes and the dried and powdered roots of iris and sweet flag." (*Nostradamus*, Francis X. King, St. Martin's Press)

Francis X. King went on to say how such a potion couldn't have helped patients at all, but what probably did was just the fact that Nostradamus disapproved of many of the terrible "cures" of his day and therefore didn't use them, much to the benefit of his patients.

The fact is, it is sensible to be cynical of anything spoken by the mouth or penned by the hand of a human being. Sadly, this includes all of documented history. How do we *know* that what we have been taught about the past is indeed fact? We can only *believe* it was so. It is even wise to approach the Bible with a desire for proof that it is indeed the Word of God, and not the words of mere men. The Book itself says "prove *all* things." Faith in the Scriptures should not be irrational conviction. It should be founded on what is considered to be trustworthy. Is the Bible *worthy* of our trust? This is something we will look at in depth further on in this publication.

Chapter Seven
Farewell New York

As stated earlier, there are some remarkable prophecies of Nostradamus. Here is what is commonly accepted as his vision of World War Two:

The machines of flying fire
Will come to trouble the great commander of the besieged:
Inside there will be such sedition
That the overthrown will be in despair. (C6 Q34)

Here are the periscopes of Nazi submarines:

Where he thought to breed famine
There will come plenty,
While the eye of the sea watches like a greedy dog;
For one to the other will give oil, wheat. (C4 Q15)

Here are the fighter pilots:

They will think they have seen the sun at night,
When they see the pig half-man:
Noise, song, battle, fighting in the sky perceived:
And brute beasts will be heard to speak. (C1 Q64)

The seer also saw submarines:

...when the fleet can swim under water. C3 Q13)

It is also interesting to note that Leonardo da Vinci foresaw and even *sketched* the helicopter. He predicted the machine gun, the parachute--which he called the "tent of linen." He formulated Isaac Newton's laws of motion well over a century before Newton was born. The Franciscan monk Roger Bacon (1220-1293) even foresaw what could be interpreted as ocean liners, cars, planes and deep sea divers.

In 1899, H.G. Wells predicted automatic doors and a time when religion would be marketed "like soap powder." In 1875, Jules Verne foretold when buildings would be a thousand feet high, and spoke of air and underwater travel.

So long New York
If you think Nostradamus spoke the truth, you had better stay clear of New York:

The Secrets of Nostradamus Exposed

At forty-five degrees the sky will burn,
Fire approaches the great new city,
Instantly a great, scattered flame shall leap up.

(C6 Q97)

New York, "the new city," will be bombarded by missiles that will "burn" the sky at forty-five degrees. New York is situated between the fortieth and forty-fifth parallels. (*Predictions*)

Jeane Dixon

Perhaps you have faith in Jeane Dixon, America's most famous psychic. She is the woman who supernaturally heard of the coming assassination of President Kennedy, and who many believe was mentioned by Nostradamus in prophecy.

As a child she wanted to be an actress or a nun. Instead she became a living prophetess. She has been called "Washington's phenomenal seeress." She daily received avalanches of fan mail from her world-syndicated horoscope column. Despite her deep involvement in the occult, she aspired "to spread the Christian Gospel" into as many homes as possible. Every morning, she carried her deeply felt convictions to Mass after rising to recite the Twenty-third Psalm from her window." (Ibid)

She had her palm read when she was only eight

years old, and the mystic told her that she herself would become a great mystic. It was at that meeting that she was given a crystal ball. Perhaps it was then that she also picked up a familiar spirit which evidently stayed with her. Here are the details from her biography:

"...The gypsy woman continued, 'Your child, madam, is designed for great things. In both her hands she has all the markings of a great mystic.' Lost in deep thought, she turned around and disappeared into her wagon. When she returned she had a ball in her hand--a crystal ball. 'Here, my little one,' she said softly, placing the ball gently into my outstretched hands. 'Take it--tell me what you see.'"

After the child described a rocky coast, a turbulent sea and giant waves, the gypsy was overjoyed and said,

"Keep the ball. It is yours. It can do more in your hands than in mine!" *My Life and Prophecies* (William Morrow and Company, 1969)

Mrs. Dixon, like Nostradamus was never at a loss for words when it came to predictions. She also (as does the Bible) prophesied of the coming of the anti-Christ, earthquakes, the second coming of Christ, etc.

But didn't her occultic practices--her horoscopes, her psychic powers, etc., conflict with her Roman Catholic faith? Not at all. She, like Nostradamus, saw no conflict.

When questions have been asked about Nostradamus's conversion, one expert explains why he thought the prophet was a sincere Catholic:

"There seems to be no good reason to doubt Nostradamus's Catholicism--although, like a number of other occultists throughout the centuries, he appears to have found his faith quite compatible with the practice of ritual magic and other forbidden arts." *Nostradamus*, Francis X. King, page 25, St. Martin's press).

Indeed Jeane Dixon says of her well-known horoscope column:

"The science of astrology was taught me as a child by Father Henry, a consecrated, dedicated Jesuit priest at Loyola University in California, and it was through his teachings as well as his exemplary goodness that I came to believe it is possible also to

help people through such astrological knowledge."
My Life and Prophecies (William Morrow and
Company, 1969)

As with Nostradamus and other psychics, Jean
Dixon was convinced beyond a shadow of a doubt
that God was speaking through her. In the Prologue
to her biography, she says:

"Each of us has a talent that functions as a primary
channel of communication between the Higher
Power and ourself...I believe that a like spirit that
worked through the Biblical prophets Isaiah and
John the Baptist works through some of us.

"Revelations are signs of the will of God, and
not the will of man. When *God* reveals a future
event through a revelation, nothing man can do will
change it. The Lord gives a revelation to anyone
whom He chooses, when He chooses, and how He
chooses. A revelation has nothing whatsoever to do
with extra sensory perception. It is God revealing
His will, and when He chooses to use me as a
channel for His revelation, I listen, I see, and I
feel..." (Ibid)

Also like Nostradamus, she has much to say
about the Bible, about the church, God, prayer,
etc., but comparatively little about the person of

Jesus Christ. Yet the test as to whether or not someone is speaking for God, is their conviction as to who Jesus Christ is. A demon spirit will deny the incarnation of the Savior. It will refuse to acknowledge Him for who He is. Let's look again at the First Epistle of John and the verses that follow:

"Beloved, do not believe every spirit, but test the spirits, whether they are God; because many false prophets have gone into the world."

How do we "test" the spirit to see if it is of God? Is it a false prophet--a demonic spirit or is it the Spirit of God that is speaking through the prophet? The following verse tells us how:

"By this you know the Spirit of God: Every spirit that confesses that Jesus Christ has come in the flesh is of God. And every spirit that does not confess that Jesus Christ has come in the flesh is not of God. And this is the spirit of anti-Christ, which you have heard was coming, and is now already in the world" (1 John 4:2-3, italics added).

In fact, knowledge of who Jesus is, *is the very rock upon which the Church is built*. When Jesus asked Peter who he thought He was, Peter answered, "Thou art the Christ, the Son of the Living God." Jesus answered, "Blessed art thou Peter, for flesh and blood hath not revealed this unto you, but My Father Who is in Heaven. Thou art Peter, and upon this rock will I build My Church" (Matthew 16:18). The "foundation" of the Church is Jesus Christ (1 Corinthians 3:11).

Look now at Jeane Dixon's words and receive insight into the humble mind of a psychic:

"Quickly I turned and, re-entering the drawing room, spoke to the little dove in a soft, caressing tones. 'Come here, little one,' I coaxed. 'Come and let me hold you.'

"Just as though he understood my words, he circled around again and flew directly to me, touching down gently on my right hand. With the dove in the palm of my hand I slowly turned and walked back onto the terrace, talking to him softly. The dove's unusual response to me attracted everyone's attention. All conversation ceased; every eye was on us, aware that something was happening beyond what they were seeing.

"The dove nestled in my hand and watched my face intently as if afraid of missing one single word. His tiny black eyes never wavering but kept looking at me with great serenity. Was he telling me something? I was not sure, but I stopped talking nevertheless and tried to concentrate with him on whatever his coming was meant to convey."

This dove was apparently an omen. It was significant of the Holy Spirit. Look now at what happens when she tunes in to the spirit:

"My mind's eye can often look deep into the far beyond, and my mind's ear can sometimes tune in to the far sounds of heaven, but this time I not only saw and heard, but felt--God omnipresent, God controlling and God directing every capsule of time and space. Gone from my consciousness was the reception, gone were the people...I was alone with the Eternal One, and felt reverently awed, and was experiencing again that beautiful unearthly quiet in the vast unending space of the great beyond.

"Hardly conscious of moving, I stepped onto the terrace, the dove in my hand. People moved little, off to one side, and to me it seemed as if the Red Sea were parting again. I was as if I were not me--a mortal--any more, but a spirit of consciousness--off somewhere in vast, unbounded space, looking down the years at things to come. I could feel the earth shake and tremble underfoot. Then it seemed as though the world had stopped rotating on its axis.

I saw that this century there will be many...earth-quakes." (Ibid)

Move over Moses. Here comes Jeane with a dove in hand, complete with the Red Sea parting, drifting through the galaxy, voyaging through time. *This was no small happening*. The earth shook beneath her feet, the world stopped turning on its axis...and what does she prophecy? What great life-shattering truth is the spirit going to speak to her about?--*earthquakes!* That was kinda predictable. Good old earthquakes. They never fail to impress those who are ignorant of the Bible. The dove wasn't the only thing she had in the palm of her hand.

Here are some more of her inspiring and power-ful prophecies, published in, *Predictions* (Fisher and Commins) back in 1980:

-- *A comet will strike the earth in the middle of the 1980's, causing potentially disastrous earthquakes and tidals* (many thought Halley's Comet which appeared in 1986 would be a fulfillment of C2 Q26's *In the heavens fire seen, a long spark run-ning*. However, Halley's Comet turned out to be a fizzer, unable to be seen with the naked eye).

-- Many will "die like ants" in the 1980's as a result of germ warfare unleashed on the Western world by Red China in alliance with Asian and African nations.

-- More than a dozen African nations will take sides in a great war on that continent in 1987--the African equivalent of World War Two.

-- Intelligent life will be discovered on a sister planet "exactly on the other side of the sun."

-- The United States will have its first woman president in the 1980s.

Jeane Dixon should have thanked God that she wasn't born in Bible times, where her ramblings may have been silenced by a rock group.

Even her "remarkable" prediction of President Kennedy's assassination wanes a little in the light of the following:

"The idea that whoever was to be elected president in 1960 was destined to die in office had been, as it were 'in the air' ever since President Roosevelt's death in the office in the spring of 1944. This was because, as those interested in numerology had

111

noted at the time of Roosevelt's death, since 1840 every US president who had been elected to office in the year ending with zero had died in office."
(*Nostradamus*, Francis X. King, page 73, St. Martin's Press)

The Bible warns that in these days there would be an increase in people who explored the psychic world. It says that they will listen to "seducing spirits and doctrines of devils" (Timothy 4:1). The same verse even predicts that those who do so will also have had a connection to the Christian faith.

There is a fast buck and instant recognition for those who can guess an unborn child's sex ten times in a row. Each year, a million psychics give a million prophecies about a million things. When one hits the mark, it makes headlines and establishes cliental. Modern psychics are nothing but glorified fortune cookies. While you are looking for your fortune, they are *making* theirs, and there are plenty of hungry customers who willingly part with their dollars to swallow their mindless morsels.

Here are some more predictions from those who, like Nostradamus have emptied their minds to allow spirits to babble through them:

Irene Hughes (who has been called, "America's

self-proclaimed first lady of the parasciences,"
from, *Predictions*--1980, page 102):

-- *Some form of nuclear war will break out within
ten years.*
-- *A United States president will die in office in the
1980s.*
-- *An oncoming ice age will be "very evident" by
1983 and fully upon us by 1989.*
-- *The next pope will be assassinated and cardinals
will rule the church until the papacy is no more
in 1989.*
-- *New York will be destroyed.*

Evidently she was a fan of Nostradamus.

Edgar Cayce

Edgar was called "America's Most Mysterious
Man." He was a psychic who would lie on his
couch in his study, fold his arms across his chest,
close his eyes and go into a state of self-hypnosis.
This is a pleasant way of saying he went into a demonic trance. He became so famous in the 1930's
and 40's that 1500 requests for readings poured in
daily. Despite the fame and fortune, he was a quiet
man "who studied his Bible daily." (Ibid, page 75)

Amazingly, Edgar Cayce predicted the "creation

of the State of Israel." So does the Bible. He also predictably predicted earthquakes and famines, etc. He foretold of the destruction of New York (another fan of Nostradamus), and like Nostradamus, he regularly used biblical phrases in his prophecies. In fact, the authors of *Predictions* were amazed by his projections, saying they were,

"...sprinkled with words such as Ye, Yea, Thy and Hath...they sound positively Biblical at times."

Edgar was a family man. He believed in Hinduism's reincarnation, drank alcohol, smoked like a train and "enjoyed the company of attractive women." Despite his occult activity, he was "a devout Christian" (Ibid). He died in 1945, but believed he would humbly rejoin us in 1998, possibly as "a liberator of the world." He certainly did *lie* on his couch.

Simon Says

Here is what psychic Simon Alexander says would happen after the 1980s:

-- ...*there will already have been, in the late 1980s, a nuclear disaster in the States which wiped out an entire community.*

-- *South Africa will cease to exist.*
-- *Pornography will be a thing of the past.*
-- *Exploited sex will not be at all popular.*
-- *No "super civilization" will be discovered on other planets, but contact will be made with a backward, humanoid form of life.* (Ibid, p. 104)

Perhaps this "backward humanoid form of life" could give us some clear guidance. Maybe they will turn out to be the comparatively intelligent life the world has been searching for.

Chapter Eight
More Prophecies

There are three types of people in the world--
those that can count, and those that can't. The
world is full of experts who make deductions, but
their conclusion seems to be missing something.
They don't add up. This is the case with the ac-
counts of Nostradamus's exhumation, his "bril-
liance" in the medical field, and with the "Hitler"
and other interpretations.

Take for example the much celebrated claim that
the British used the prophecies of Nostradamus for
propaganda during the Second World War. Did this
really happen? Once again, it is based on truth, but
colored a little:

"Nostradamus's persistent influence rests partly
with his ambiguity: For years, people of various
persuasions have managed to read something mean-
ingful into his cryptic verses. During World War

Two both Germany and Great Britain en-listed the

© Softkey Int'l

Did Nostradamus predict the outcome of the Second World War?

seer for their own ends. 'Nostradamus Predicts the Course of the War' is the English title of a pamphlet produced by British intelligence in March of 1943; the document was meant to cause consternation in the enemy's homeland by predicting Hitler's doom. The Third Reich already had come up with Nostradamus adaptions of its own and planned to airlift into France copies of selected quatrains that supposedly forecast German victory. It appears the leaflets were never used, however, perhaps because of France's quick surrender, and the small number of British pamphlets smuggled into Germany had no appreciable effect." *Visions & Prophecies*, page 20 (Time-life Books)

One More Pope

Nostradamus predicted that the pope before the year 2,000 would be the last.

During the 20th Century and earlier, many experts believed that Nostradamus said there would be only one more Pope before the year 2,000.

Another clairvoyant priest (Saint Malachie) said the same thing way back in the year 1140:

> *In the final persecution of the Holy*
> *Roman Church there will reign Peter*
> *the Roman, who will feed his flock*
> *among many tribulations: after which*
> *the seven-hilled City will be destroyed*
> *and the dreadful Judge will judge the people.*

The seven-hilled City referred to by Malachie is apparently Rome. Francis King explains:

"The expression 'dreadful Judge' is usually taken as a reference to the Last Judgment, when the living and the resurrected dead are to be sentenced to either eternal damnation or given the reward of eternal bliss. But it could mean a judgment of a different sort--some world-shattering event, or series of events, which destroys the Church. In either case, if Nostradamus and Malachie are in concordance, then the next Pope is going to be the last." (*Nostradamus*, Francis X. King, page 83, St. Martin's Press, 1994)

This interpretation is confirmed by the authors of, *Man, Myth & Magic*:

"Destruction of Rome...the last one will assume the name carefully avoided by all popes to date, and will be known as Peter of Rome..." *Man, Myth & Magic*, Vol. 23, page 3131 (Marshall Cavendish Corporation, New York).

Move Over Napoleon

While many apply the following prophecy to Napoleon (the first of three anti-Christs, Hitler being the second), it is said that the helmet far better fits Heinrich Himmler. This human monster apparently died while talking to someone:

The dart from heaven will make its journey,
Death while speaking, a great execution;
The stone in the tree, a proud race abased,
Talk of a human monster, purge and expiation.
(C2 Q70)

The Swastika

Most of us associate the swastika with the Nazis. However, it was long in use before Hitler picked it up. It has been used in Hinduism and was also used in Germany before the First World War as a symbol of the mythological god Thor. Hitler reversed the position of the arms in the 1920s and employed it as the badge of his corrupt movement. Nostradamus saw the swastika:

The great Priest of the Party of Mars
Who will subjugate the Danube
The cross harried by the crook...

He Saw the Mark, and Lady Di

What did Nostradamus see in the 20th Century? Here is Reagan, and Gorbachev (complete with the birthmark on his head--last line):

U.S. President Ronald Reagon and Soviet President Gorbachev, December, 1987.

The Secrets of Nostradamus Exposed

One day the two great leaders will be friends,
Their great power will be seen to grow:
The New Land will be at the height of its power,
To the man of blood the number is reported.

(C2 Q89)

He even saw Princess Diana (who will make it to her 73rd birthday):

She who was cast out will return to reign,
Her enemies found among conspirators.
More than ever will her reign be triumphant.
At three and seventy death is very sure. (C6 Q74)

If Di doesn't die on the due departure date, then it will be claimed that it wasn't Nostradamus that was at fault, but our *inaccurate interpretation* of his prophecy, thus keeping his credibility intact. This is the reason his plausibility is still undamaged in the minds of so many. His prophecies are so mystical, so ambiguous, that if the cap doesn't fit one head, there are plenty of other heads to try it on.

Space Exploration, AIDS and the Net

Here is a description of a manned space station:

Samarobin one hundred leagues from the hemisphere

The Secrets of Nostradamus Exposed

They will live without law, exempt from politics.
                              (C6 Q34)

Here is the outbreak of the AIDS virus:

The dreadful war which is prepared in the west,
The following year the pestilence will come,
So horrible that neither young nor old. (C9 Q55)

This quatrain is a computer virus:

A thing existing without any senses
Will cause its own death to happen through arti-
fice... (C1 Q22)

The submarine-launched Trident missile during
the Gulf War was even seen by the prophet:

When the travelling earthly and watery fish
Is thrown upon the shore by a great wave
Its strange from wild and horrifying
From the sea its enemies soon reach the walls.
                              (C1 Q29)

While some interpreters see the following
quatrain as a clear allusion to the United States,
expert Francis X. King (X. for Xpert) explains--

"these lines refer to the first hot-air balloons":

There will go forth from Mont
Gaulfier and the Aventine one
Who through a whole will give
Information to the army. (C5 Q57)

Somehow I think he may be onto something. It does seem to be something to do with hot air.

One trump-card of Nostradamifites is the incredible prediction of the Great Fire of London. The prophet not only gave the date of the fire (1666), but he named London, and gave other details that English history tells us confirmed his words to a cup of tea. How could this be? Here is a possible answer:

"Still other quatrains that have been considered farsighted may actually refer to contemporary events with which Nostradamus should have been familiar. Skeptics cite the quatrain that purportedly depicts the Great Fire of London, down to the date, 'twenty-three the sixes,' or 1666. (To arrive at the year, believers multiply twenty by three, add a pair of sixes, and note that it was common in Nostradamus's time to omit the first digits of a date.) The verse's forecast of a fall of a lady from a high place has traditionally been interpreted as a reference to St. Paul's Church, which was so ravished by the flames, it was torn down. But skeptics suggest that Nostradamus more likely referred to Queen Mary of England, known as Bloody Mary, who was at the time executing numbers of heretics, often in groups of six. Although Mary did not die until 1558, after the verse was printed, it would not have been particularly insightful in that turbulent era to predict a ruler's downfall or death." *Visions & Prophecies, page 20* (Time-life Books)

Goodbye California

If you still have faith in the prophecies of Nostradamus, sink your faith-filled teeth into the following yet to be realized predictions:

Towards the south there will be a great drought. An earthquake will be reported from the bottom of Asia, Corinth, and Ephesus in an unstable and troubled state... (C3 Q3)

For several nights the earth will shake,
In the spring two great efforts together; Corinth and Ephesus will swim in two seas... (C2 Q52)

The trembling of the earth at Mortara, the tin

islands of St. George are half sunk... (C9 Q31)

Here's the interpretation from John Hogue:

"...Next comes the long awaited superquake in the San Andreas fault which will rock the west coast of America. Sea water will flood into the Southern Californian deserts from the gulf of California as the west coast breaks away from the mainland." (*Nostradamus and the Millennium*, page 162)

This was to happen in the "mid 1990's." My home is in Southern California, and as far as I know it is still part of the mainland of the U.S.

The interpretation continues:

"By the mid-1990's a second wave of superquakes is generally foreseen. By then the western United States will have vanished or broken up into islands. East Africa will split into three pieces. South America and Tierra del Fuego also split apart. New York City and Florida will be flooded as new continent-sized islands rise off the Caribbean, the submerged coast of Southern California and the South Pacific. New Zealand, Australia and Virginia in the United States, are seen by modern psychics as safe areas."

New Zealand is situated right on the "Pacific rim" (the name given to the rim of faults upon which 60% of the world's earthquakes occur. New Zealand sits at the bottom of the rim). One quake there killed more than 30 people.

Other ace interpreters warned us that in the future, Russia would unite with America and triumph over the East after 27 years of nuclear war. This Third World War would be worse than all other wars put together and would begin sometime between 1981 and 1999.

The same authorities (commenting on C3 Q84 and C2 Q41 on a TV documentary made back in 1979, called "Nostradamus--Life, Prophecies and Mystique") said:

"These two quatrains clearly describe the destruction of Rome, probably by a nuclear blast. And if we refer to the figures acquired earlier, it seems safe to assume that sometime before the year 1995, the Pope will have to leave Rome, because the great city is devastated by an atomic bomb."

No wonder, after spending $20 million of the American tax payer's money, the CIA decided in 1995 to drop psychics as a means of intelligence. *They didn't get any*. It took them an incredible 20 years to figure out that 80% of what the psychics told them was totally false:

"One Pentagon consultant working at SRI International wrote a ten page report predicting a massive air attack on Washington during one of Reagan's State of the Union addresses...he (another psychic) became convinced there was a Martian colony hidden beneath the New Mexico desert." *Newsweek* (November 11, 1995 page 50)

Future Joys

So, what wonderful things has humanity to look forward to in the immediate future? Here is the future according to Nostradamus:

The great famine which I feel approaching
Will often recur and then become universal:
So great will it be, and so long will it last
That they will eat woodland roots and drag children from the breast. (C1 Q67)

Here is the exciting interpretation from Francis X. King:

"...it may be that Nostradamus was prophesying a famine of such severity that cannibalism will be practiced throughout the entire world!" (*Nostrad-*

The Secrets of Nostradamus Exposed

amus, Francis X. King, page 98, St. Martin's Press)

Chapter Nine
Prophetic
Phenomenon

A friend stopped at the side of a freeway in Florida, and stood by a man whose car was billowing out black smoke. The vehicle had caught fire and became engulfed in flames. The man escaped being incinerated in his own car, and acknowledged that it was the hand of God that saved him from such a terrible death.

As fire trucks arrived and dowsed the flames, my friend spoke of the transient nature of this life, and quoted from the Bible about how only God is everlasting.

When the fire was out, all that was left of the vehicle was a burned out, blackened, dripping shell. The firemen then opened the trunk and removed a box of smoking and charred books. As they took each of the old books from the box, only one was completely clean and untouched by the flames and smoke. Only one was preserved...the Bible.

Down through the ages, men have tried to destroy the Book that accused them of sin. While the Bible is the world's most loved book, it is also the world's most hated. Yet, despite the malignity directed at it, despite the ages that have passed, it remains unscathed to this day as the world's all-time best seller.

Try an experiment. Say something that someone will quote tomorrow. I don't mean say something that Shakespeare or some other great mind of the past penned, but something original, from your own heart, and see if anyone even *remembers* what you said tomorrow, let alone quotes you.

There is no record of Jesus Christ writing down His words, but there is a record of Him saying, "Heaven and earth will pass away, but My words will never pass away." Today, *after two thousand years* His words are not only preserved, but hundreds of millions live by them as their very code of life.

You say, "But the same applies for great men of the past, such as Buddha, Muhammad, etc." Perhaps, but there is one big difference. Look at the following statements of Jesus Christ and tell me if they are the words of a sane man:

"I am the way, the truth and the life. No one comes to the Father, but by Me." (John 14:6)

Here is a man, claiming not only that *He* is the way, the truth and the life, but He says that He alone is the exclusive way to God. No one, including all other religions (according to this Man) can get to God but through Him.

"Do not marvel not at this; for the hour is coming in which all who are in the graves will hear His voice." (John 5:28)

Jesus Christ is referring to Himself. He is saying that all the billions that have died down through the ages are going to hear *His* voice. *His* voice will raise them from the dead to stand before God in judgment. (John 5:29)

His distinctive words have been preserved for us to read in the Bible. They show us that this was no ordinary man. Add to this His prophetic statements, and we are left with an intellectual dilemma. Either He was God in human form, or He was a nut. How many people would have given the words of Nostradamus serious thought if he claimed that whoever saw him, saw God; that he was going to raise all humanity from the dead; that the salvation of the entire human race depended on the world's attitude to him?

I hate instruction books. I would rather attempt to put an appliance together myself. When things don't come together, I *then* go to the instruction book.

Statistics tell us that each year an incredible two million people get infections while they are in hospital. Of these, 60,000 people actually die of infections. What is the answer to this terrible dilemma? We are told that if hospital staff simply wash their hands in running water, it would stop this massive waste of human life.

It is only in the last hundred or so years that we have understood that bacteria lives on hands, and that it can be transferred to others. This is the number one reason why so many women died at childbirth for so many years.

It is a tragic shortcoming in human nature to only read the Instruction Book when things go wrong. God gave us the Book, but we would rather try and put things together ourselves, to our own terrible detriment.

In the year 1490 B.C., God told Israel through Moses about the washing of hands in running water because of the contamination of disease:

"And whomsoever he toucheth that hath the issue, and hath not rinsed his hands in water, he shall wash his clothes, and bathe himself in water, and be unclean until the evening. And the vessel of earth, that he toucheth which hath the issue, shall be broken: and every vessel of wood shall be rinsed in water. And when he that hath an issue is cleansed of his issue; then he shall number himself seven days for his cleansing, and wash his clothes, and bathe his flesh in running water, and shall be clean." (Leviticus 15:11-13)

This is just one case of the many that we will look at to show that this book we call the Bible, is no ordinary book.

Authentic Prophets

There are prophets of the Bible who predicted that Russia would sweep down upon Israel and seek to destroy it as a nation. The credibility of these prophets was not judged upon how often they were right, but how often they were wrong. The qualification in those days was a life and death issue. False prophets were stoned.

Too many of the masses are wide-eyed and naive, and have been led down the path of gullible's travels. As said earlier, I want to know if some-

135

thing is totally trustworthy before I will put my faith in it. So I'm going to give you information for you to weigh within your mind. How can you know whether these writings are dependable? Is there any way of conclusively finding out if they are supernaturally inspired? Were they written by man or by God?

When a man drafts a letter, does he write it or does his pen? Obviously, *he* writes the letter, and the pen is the tool he uses. The claim of the men who penned the Bible, is that it was *God* who did the writing, while they were the tools He used. If the Bible is the Word of our Creator, and its claim that immortality is a free gift, then we would be fools not to at least give it a fleeting glance. But if it is merely an historical narrative, the writings of men, it must be exposed as being fraudulent, as millions have been deceived by it.

The irony of the Christian faith is that it *seems* to be intellectual suicide, but proves to be the ultimate intellectual challenge. What we will do to begin with, is look at four sets of remarkable information:

1/ Scientific facts
2/ General information

3/ Prophetic realization
4/ Politically prophetic fulfillment

Before we do, realize that the Bible was written by 40 men, over a very long period of time--1600 years, beginning in the year 1500 B.C. Its continual claim is that these men were motivated by God (2 Peter 1:21).

Scientific Facts

At a time when science taught that the earth sat on a large animal or an immense giant (1500 B.C.), the Bible spoke of the earth's free float in space:

"He...hangeth the earth upon nothing." (Job 26:7)

Perhaps the translators are twisting the original language, or perhaps I am interpreting the verse for more than it says. In the original the wording "hangeth" is *talah* meaning "to suspend." The word "earth" is *erets* which is "earth," and "nothing" is *beliymah* which means "nothing whatever." So to be more literal, the verse says: "He suspends the earth upon nothing whatever."

For many years, this verse would have been ample evidence that the Bible contained an error-- right up until we discovered that there is no gravity in space and that the earth is suspended over nothing whatever.

The prophet Isaiah tells us that the earth is round: "It is He who sitteth upon the circle of the earth" (Isaiah 40:22).

In the original language, the word *circle* means "circle." The secular world got around to discovering this 2400 years later, although history tells us that Christopher Columbus was aware of it when he discovered the new world.

Not too many people realize that radio waves and light waves are two different forms of the same thing. God broadcast this fact to His listeners in the year 1500 B.C.: "Canst thou send lightnings, that they may go and say unto thee, Here we are?" (Job 38:35). Who would have believed that light could be *sent* and actually *speak*?

This was first realized in 1864 when "the British scientist James Clerk Maxwell suggested that electricity and light waves were two forms of the same thing" (*Modern Century Illustrated Encyclopedia* Volume 12).

The Book of Job is very specific in its description of light saying, "Where is the way where light dwells" (Job 38:19). Contemporary society has only just uncovered that light has a "way," involving motion traveling at 186,000 miles per second.

Science has now ascertained that stars send out radio waves. These are received on earth as a high pitch. God mentioned this in Job 38:7 "... when the morning stars sang together..."

When science can only guess as to why the dinosaur disappeared, the Bible sheds light on the subject. In Job 40:15-24, God Himself describes the largest of all the creatures He made. He gives details of a massive animal which is herbivorous (plant-eating), has a tail like a very large tree, having its strength in its hips, very strong bones, a habitat among trees, able to consume large amounts of water, and being of very great height.

Then the Scriptures say, "... He that made him can make his sword to approach unto him." In other words, God brought extinction to this massive creature.

Science is merely a pitiful attempt to discover the works of God. Notice the word "uncannily" in the following quote and ask yourself why it's there:

"Most cosmologists (scientists who study the structure and evolution of the universe) agree that the Genesis account of creation, in imagining an initial void, may be uncannily close to the truth." (*Time*, December 1976)

The word smacks of an intellectual condescension, at the very thought that the Bible could contain any scientific truth. Much as they would not have it so, it contains more truth then the Sahara Desert has sand.

We are informed that science expresses the universe in five terms: time, space, matter, power and motion. The Book of Genesis Chapter 1 revealed such truths to the Hebrews way back in 1450 BC:

"In the beginning (time) God created the Heaven (space) and the earth (matter)...And the Spirit (power) of God moved (motion) upon the face of the waters."

In the next chapter, we will look at further evidence to substantiate the fact that the Bible is more than just a history book, and the implications for humanity.

Chapter Ten
Divine Prophecies

In the previous chapter we examined some of the remarkable scientific facts in the Scriptures. Now we will continue by looking at more general elements.

In Genesis Chapter 6, God furnished Noah with the dimensions of a one million, three hundred thousand cubic square foot ark he was to build. In 1609, at Hoon in Holland, a ship was built after that same pattern, something that revolutionized shipbuilding. By the year 1900, every large ship on the high seas was definitely inclined towards the proportions of the ark (as verified by "Lloyd's Register of Shipping" in the, *World Almanac*).

God asked Job a strange question in Job 38:22. He said, "Hast thou entered into the treasures of the snow?"

This didn't make too much sense to us until the advent of the microscope, revealing the incredible beauty of snow crystals. Every single snowflake has its own unique shape. There are billions, and yet it is said that not one of the amazing patterns are the same.

Two prophecies (Genesis 49:1,20 & Deuteronomy 33:24), written around 3,000 years B.C. combine to tell us:"In the latter days...Asher...let him dip his foot in oil."

As one studies a map of the tribe of Asher, it perfectly resembles a foot poised to dip. In 1935, the Great International Iraq Petroleum Enterprise opened precisely at the base of the foot, pumping a million gallons of oil a day to the Haifa harbor.

In Genesis Chapter 16, God said that Ishmael (the "progenitor of the Arab race," *Time*, April 4, 1988) would be a "wild man, and every man's hand will be against him; and he shall dwell in the presence of all his brethren." Four thousand years later, who could repudiate the fact that this prophecy is being fulfilled in the Arab race? The Arabs and the Jews are "brethren" having the same ancestors. The whole cause of Middle East strife is because they are dwelling together.

In Isaiah 66:7-8 (700 BC), the Prophet gives a strange prophecy:

"Before she travailed, she brought forth; before her pain came, she was delivered of a man-child; who hath heard such a thing? Who hath seen such things? Shall the earth be made to bring forth in one day? Or shall a nation be born at once? For as soon as Zion travailed, she brought forth her children."

In 1922, the League of Nations gave Great Britain the mandate (political authority) over Palestine. On May 14, 1948, Britain withdrew her mandate, and the nation of Israel was "born in a day." There are more than 25 Bible prophecies concerning Palestine that have been literally fulfilled. Probability computer estimations conclude that the likelihood of these being accidentally fulfilled are more than one chance in 33 million.

In 1905, Scotland Yard in England launched into a new era of scientific detection. At a murder trial, Detective Inspector Stockley Collins explained to the jury that skin patterns could furnish up to 20 characteristics on a single finger. Over 10 years, he had examined a million fingerprints and never found more than three identical characteristics on the fingers of any two people. They discovered that every single person has a seal, an imprint on their hand, hence fingerprint evidence now taken at crime scenes. The Book of Job tells us this amazing fact many years before Scotland Yard discovered it: "He (God) sealeth up the hand of every man, that all men may know his work." (Job 37:7)

In spring of 1947, the Dead Sea Scrolls were discovered. These manuscripts were copies of large portions of the Old Testament, a thousand years older than any other existing copies. Study of the scrolls has revealed that the Bible didn't change in content down through the ages as so many skeptics had surmised.

Many times I have heard the statement that the Bible is "full of mistakes." Over the years I have spent thousands of hours searching the Scriptures, and I can't find them. There are numbers of *seeming* contradictions, but experience has taught me that if we think there are mistakes, *we* are actually the ones who are mistaken, not God.

In the past I have publicly offered thousands of dollars to anyone who can prove to me that there is even one mistake in the Word of God, and never found any serious contenders. I have spoken in prestigious universities such as Yale, California State, Arizona, Utah, Berkeley and others, on the subject of the Bible. Those who say it is full of errors have never taken the time to study it. They merely *believe* what others have told them. They prefer to have faith in the word of man, rather than discover for themselves if the Bible is the Word of God. Not many thieves search for policemen.

Prophetic Facts

Bible Law states that the prophet of God must be 100% accurate in his prophecy. If he turned his hearers away from the God revealed in Scripture, he was to be put to death. Nostradamus would have certainly been stoned to death as a false prophet. If the Bible is the Book of the perfect Creator, its prophecies will be perfectly accurate.

There are certain signs we are instructed to look for, which will warn us of the coming Day when Almighty God reveals Himself as the Great Judge of humanity. This is known as the "Great and terrible Day of the Lord." It will be when His everlasting Kingdom comes to earth, and His will will be done on earth, "as it is in Heaven."

Look now at the faultless description the Bible gives of this day in which we live:

False Bible teachers will be money hungry. They will be smooth talkers, have many followers, and will slur the Christian faith (2 Peter 2:1-3).

Homosexuality will be increasingly evident at the end of the age (2 Timothy 3:3). At present, there are reported to be more than seventeen million homosexuals in the United States of America, and despite the loss of many thousands through the tragedy of AIDS, they are still growing in numbers. The fruit of their lifestyle has hardly deterred their zeal for homosexual practices.

Another sign is that earthquakes will increase in frequency (Matthew 24:7). Scientists estimate that there are an incredible one million earthquakes each year, with as many as twenty going on concurrently around the world. Between the years 1940 and 1950 there were four "killer" earthquakes. Then between

© Softkey Int'l

Rescue workers look for bodies trapped between collapsed double-deck freeways after a major earthquake in California in 1989.

1950 and 1960 they more than doubled in number to nine. From the years 1960 to 1970 there were thirteen. Between 1970 and 1980 there was a four-fold increase to fifty-six. Then from 1980 to 1990 *there were seventy four*.

There will be an increase in heart attacks brought on by stress, resulting in death (Luke 21:26). Who could deny that fact? Almost every night on television, advertisements remind us about our intake of salt, cholesterol and fats, and give statistics so frightening they could easily cause heart-failure.

Nations are rising against nations and ethnic groups fighting each other.

Many wars will erupt (Matthew 24:6). Over the past 6,000 years, humanity has only managed an estimated 260 years of peace. There have been over 100 wars since 1945, with over 54,800,000 deaths from the Second World War alone. There are so many wars, hostilities, and skirmishes going on at any given moment around the world, they don't even merit any mention on the news.

The Bible warns that these times will reveal an increase in the occult (1 Timothy 4:1). In the United States there is enough business to keep 10,000 astrologers working full-time, and an additional 175,000 astrologers working part-time. Halloween is as popular as Christmas. Horoscopes are in almost every newspaper, with many top-selling books, movies and rock groups extolling satanism and other occultic activities.

Perhaps you are not feeling well. For just $75 an hour you can have a psychic send "healing thoughts" to you from the other side of the country. Or you could call "The Witches of Salem Network," because "if you like talking to psychics...you'll love talking to witches."

Psychics can reveal "hidden secrets about love, life, career, money, luck, marriage, health, the future and personal problems." You can even call the Reverend Johnny Love for healing power prayer. He's a "gifted spiritualist psychic." Through astrology you can "find your destiny"..."expand your horizons"...and "unleash the power."

You don't even have to leave your home to find your own Nostradamus. In the comfort of your home, you can make a connection. Your own confidential psychic can give you your own personal reading over your own personal telephone. What's more, it's free. All it will cost you is $3.99 per minute and your eternal salvation.

Many of these modern psychics, like Nostradamus, suppose that their revelations are from God. But look at what happened in the Bible when those who had a foot into the occult world, came to faith in Jesus Christ:

"Then some of the itinerant Jewish exorcists took it upon themselves to call the name of the Lord Jesus over those who had evil spirits, saying, 'We adjure you by Jesus whom Paul preaches.' Also there were seven sons of Sceva, a Jewish chief priest, who did so. And the evil spirit answered and said, 'Jesus I know, and Paul I know; but who are you?' Then the man in whom the evil spirit was leaped on them, and prevailed against them, so that they fled out of that house naked and wounded. This became known both to the Jews and Greeks dwelling in Ephesus; and fear fell on them all, and the name of the Lord Jesus was magnified. And many who had believed came confessing and telling their deeds. Also, many of those who had practiced magic brought their books together and burned them in the sight of all. And they counted up the value of them, and it totaled fifty thousand pieces of silver" (Acts 19:13-19).

As soon as they received the Holy Spirit they renounced their occult activity. Then they burned anything which gave them contact with the spirit world. This portion of scripture doesn't mention the word "divination," but in the chapters earlier, the Apostle Paul shows its origin:

"Now it happened, as we went to prayer, that a certain slave girl *possessed with a spirit of divination* met us, who brought her masters much profit by fortune-telling. This girl followed Paul and us, and cried out, saying, 'These men are the servants of the Most High God, who proclaim to us the way of salvation.' And this she did for many days. But Paul, greatly annoyed, turned and said to the spirit,

'I command you in the name of Jesus Christ to come out of her.' And he came out that very hour" Acts 16:16-18, (italics added).

The spirit that possessed the girl was attempting to promote the belief that *God* was the source of both her and Paul's message. There is nothing new under the sun.

In an effort to equate the Old Testament prophets with the occultic realm, Theodore H. Robinson, speaking of the manner in which the Spirit came upon them says:

"He might be mingling with the crowd... Suddenly something would happen to him. His eyes would become fixed, strange convulsions would seize upon his limbs, the form of his speech would change. Men would recognize that the Spirit had fallen upon him. The fit would pass, and he would tell those who stood around the things which he had seen and heard..." (*Prophecy and the Old Testament in Ancient Israel*)

There is no evidence at all of *any* of God's prophets going into "strange convulsions" or convulsions seizing "his limbs," or going into a "fit" when the Holy Spirit came upon them. I have seen many people who have been possessed by demon spirits (see, *My Friends Are Dying*, Whitaker House), and this sounds like a perfect description of a demonic manifestation.

The commands of scripture make very clear as to how we should regard the occult realm:

"Give no regard to mediums and familiar spirits; do not seek after them, to be defiled by them: I am the Lord your God" (Leviticus 19:31).

Another sign of the end of the age is that people will forsake the Ten Commandments as a moral code, committing adultery, stealing, lying, and killing (Matthew 24:12). According to the Credit Card Service Bureau, every year thieves run up charges of more than $171,000,000.00. *USA Today* reported that a survey revealed just over 50% of men have committed adultery, with women not too far behind. Nearly 25% of the boys and 16% of girls responding to a survey on rape, said it was acceptable for a man to force a woman to have sex with him if he had spent money on her. In New York, bullet-proof clothing is the latest fashion-wear for New York City children who face a dangerous trip to and from school. School blazers and other jackets fitted with bullet-proof material are providing a feeling of safety for parents who don't mind a price-tag of up to $600.

U.S. law in most states still allows the taking of the lives of the unborn children through abortion. In

Women picket an abortuary in Wichita, Kansas

1980, the high-school graduates numbered 3 million, yet in the year 1991 they, for some reason had dropped by 600,000. This co-relates with the Roe-vs-Wade legislation which legalized abortion in the mid-seventies. This was a decade which yielded the lowest birth-rate this century. In other words, because U.S. civil law ignored the Divine Law, "You shall not kill," 600,000 Americans are not around to graduate. Over one million Americans have been murdered each year through abortion.

In Pittsburgh, a young man just 18 years old, decided that he and his friends could make some extra cash by robbing an elderly couple for whom he had done some odd jobs. The gang tied the couple to chairs, then ransacked the home.

The 18 year old didn't want the victims to identify them to the police, so he decided to kill them. First, he arranged the chairs to face each other, then he cut the woman's throat. As the husband cried out and wept, the youth did the same to the old man. He then left them there in their chairs to watch each other bleed to death. This is the fruit of a society that forsakes God's Law.

The Pittsburgh murders were not isolated cases of violence. Horrific murders have become commonplace and are a biblical sign of the end of this age. Recently, in one year there were 2300 murders in the city of Los Angeles.

There will be a cold, religious system, denying God's power (2 Timothy 3:5). The Bible puts it this way, "... having a form of godliness, but denying the power thereof." In other words, they will have

154

some sort of faith in God, but they will deny the supernatural aspect both of God and of His Word. Many of the traditional churches have, especially in countries like the U.K. and Europe, become nothing more than museums, existing for the pleasure of stained-glass-gazing tourists.

Other first century Bible prophets proclaim that men will substitute fantasy in place of Christian truth (2 Timothy 4:4). This is so evident at Christmas when the birth of the Savior is lost behind the myth of Santa Claus. Also the myth of the theory of evolution is taught as fact. There is no evidence for the theory tale, yet it is espoused as gospel truth. After *Time* magazine published a cover story of "Evolution's Big Bang," one reader replied: "This report should end discussions about whether God created the earth. Now there is no way to deny the theory of evolution."

The "Big Bang" was Genesis Chapter 1, verse 1. One reader had the good sense to share his good sense. David Broussard of Dallas, Texas wrote via E-mail:

"You show the photo of a fossil of a slug-like creature and say it is the oldest known member of the line that led to humans. I think it is 'lowlife' to pass that off on others. Look at the precision of the creation around us and be honest. There had to be a Divine plan, a perfect order. The reason we don't want to acknowledge this is because then we would have to answer to the Creator who will hold us responsible for our actions. If you want to think of yourself as a descendant of a slug, fine. But don't pass it off to the rest of the world as fact."

Deadly diseases will be prevalent (Matthew 24:7). The world-wide increase in AIDS deaths is almost inestimable. Over 160,000 Americans die of cancer each year.

The fact that God once flooded the earth (the Noahic flood), will be denied (2 Peter 3:5). There is a mass of fossil evidence to prove this fact, yet it is flatly ignored by the scientific world because of its uncanny implication.

The institution of marriage will be forsaken (1 Timothy 4:3). Millions throughout the world live with each other rather than bind themselves in the commitment of holy matrimony. In 1945, 3.9% of children were born out of wedlock. By 1993, it had sky-rocketed to 31%, and climbing. Statistics tell us that we are near a 40% divorce rate for first time marriages.

There will be an increase in famines (Matthew 24:7). It is estimated that 40,000 children die every

© Softkey Int'l

A 3-year-old famine victim in Somalia's capital.

day through malnutrition. Much of the world's food shortage is caused by political policies rather than for lack of food. According to the United Nations World Health Organization one third of the world is well-fed, a third is under-fed and the other third is starving. Thirty people per minute die of starvation.

Interest in vegetarianism will increase (1 Timothy 4:3). This is no longer a counter-culture fad, but a way of life for many who think they are extending their lives by not eating meat, which God provided for that very purpose (1 Timothy 4:3-4).

There will be a cry for peace (1 Thessalonians 5:3). This has become a universal cry from the

© Softkey Int'l

There will be an international cry for peace. The possession Jerusalem will be at the center of turmoil.

poorest of peasants to prominent political polices. The possession of Jerusalem will be at the center of turmoil (Zechariah 12:3).

Knowledge (Hebrew, "science") will greatly increase (Daniel 12:4). The rate of human knowledge is said to increase 100% every two and a half years. Every 60 seconds, an estimated 2,000 typewritten pages of new knowledge are added to mankind's stockpile of facts.

There will be hypocrites in the Church (Matthew 13:25-30).

Stress will be part of living in the "latter days" (2 Timothy 3:1).

There will be an increase in religious cults (Matthew 24:11). Sects are growing at an incredible rate in the United States. To date, over 2,000 groups now claim up to 10 million members, thanks to deceptive recruiting techniques says a prominent psychologist. Margaret T. Singer of the University of California at Berkeley, who has counselled more than 700 cult members, vocalizes that many cults are becoming wealthy and, consequently, much more powerful than ever. She sings of cults moving into the suburbs, especially to private schools, where unsuspecting students are more susceptible.

Hare Krishnas are wearing wigs at airports where they collect donations and give away books, sometimes saying they are working for the YMCA. The Church of Scientology hangs posters asking parents, "Would you like your child to read better?" in an effort to lure children into the program with their parents' unknowing blessing. The Unification Church, which was headed by Reverend Sun Yung Moon, has a vast empire of convenience stores, real estate, newspapers and other businesses that make over $200 million each year, partly by hiring young people. They convert them into their religion and pay them a fraction of the minimum wage.

The Mormon Church has grown from 30 members in 1830 to where they had more than 4,000,000 way back in April, 1978. They projected that their growth would reach 8,000,000 by the year 2000. They have massive television campaigns, using advertisements that fade out the Bible and fade in the Book of Mormon. They tell you that their book goes "hand in hand with the Bible." That's not true. They teach that salvation is by works rather than by faith, something in direct opposition to the Bible. Their aim is to make the cult seem "Christian."

They will even tell you that their book will "help to give you light to know Christ." The "Christ" they speak of is not the Jesus Christ revealed in the pages of holy scripture. They believe that He was the brother of Satan, and that God has a wife. They also deny the virgin birth, teaching that God came down and had sex with Mary. There are a hundred and one other strange concepts in the cult that defy the human imagination.

The Jehovah's Witnesses are also growing at a startling rate. The group was started in 1879 by a man who claimed that he had Jehovah's divine guidance to re-establish His church on earth. They now have a world-wide membership of more than 3 million, and like most cults, claim they are the only ones on the earth who have the truth.

One of their means of obtaining converts, is to point to the fulfillment of Bible prophecy. This gives them credibility with those who are ignorant of the way of salvation. What they don't tell you, is that if you do adhere to their doctrine, you won't be allowed to associate with any ex-Jehovah's Witnesses. Neither will you be allowed to vote, salute the flag, sing the national anthem, serve the military in any way, celebrate Christmas, Mother's Day, birthdays, or other holidays, or give blood to your dying child. Nor are you allowed to think for yourself on Biblical issues or be allowed to question official "Watchtower" teachings. Neither do they tell you that they have their own version of the Bible in which they have conveniently changed major portions of Scripture; particularly those regarding the deity of Jesus Christ. They say they are Jehovah's witnesses, when if they were, they would be witnesses of Jesus Christ. Instead, they strip Him completely of His deity.

Another sign of the times will be that there will be much intimidation from nation to nation (Matthew 24:7).

The future will seem fearful to many (Luke 21:26). In January of 1991, the media reported the tragic death of a woman who was so fearful of the future, she loaded her three sons and her 3-year-old daughter into the family's minivan and drove to the secluded San Pedro point at the waterfront of the Los Angeles Harbor. She stopped the van at the red curb that faces the water and let the engine idle for a moment. Then she backed up 300 feet, turned on her high beams and put the accelerator to the floor. "There was a little screech of the tires, like burning rubber, and then ywhoooooooom," said Tom Kenourgios, a film location coordinator who was drinking coffee and reading a newspaper when he saw the van rocket into the harbor at something like 60 m.p.h.

The reason the 34-year mother took her life and the lives of her children was solely because she feared the future, not only for herself but for her children. For many, the future is hopeless. It is, for those who are ignorant of the Bible.

Humanity will become materialistic (2 Timothy 3:5).

There will be many involved in travel (Daniel 12:4). In one year U.S. citizens spent approximately $32.9 billion on international travel. In 1945, seven million Americans travelled by air. In 1994, the number had jumped to an estimated 538 million passengers.

It wasn't long ago that the fastest mode of travel was the horse. They were overtaken by trains which reached an unbelievable speed of 40 m.p.h. Nowadays jets travel at 1,000 m.p.h, with spacecraft hitting around 18,000 m.p.h. At the moment over 200 million people travel internationally each year, and with the speed increase you can be sure this number will multiply in the future. Dallas airport is planning for over 60 million passengers per year.

The Christian Gospel will be preached as a warning to all nations (Matthew 24:14).

Jesus said Christians would be hated "for His name's sake" (not for Jehovah's sake--Luke 21:17).

Many who profess to be Christians will fall away from their faith (Matthew 24:10).

There will be "signs in the sun" (Luke 21:25). This is possibly a reference to an increase in sun spots which, according to the dictionary, are "dark, irregular spots appearing periodically on the sun's surface."

There will be an increase in pestilence. There is

so much pestilence in and on the soil, it is commonplace to spray poisons on fruit trees and food crops. In fact, in the U.S. 390,000 tons of pesticides are sprayed on crops each year (*U.S. News*, November 16, 1987).

Youth will become rebellious (2 Timothy 3:2). During the late fifties and early sixties, youths exploded into new realms of rebellion, drugs and what was commonly called the "sexual revolution." The revolution wasn't just against Judeo-Christian morality, but against *all* forms of authority.

Men will mock the warning signs of the end of the age with an air of apathy saying, "These signs have always been around" (2 Peter 3:4). They fail to understand that a day to the Lord is as a thousand years to us. God is not subject to the time that He created. He can flick through time as we flick through the pages of a history book. The concept that God dwells outside of the dimension of time is too much for our minds to comprehend, but it can be proven by studying prophecy. When Nostradamus and others claimed to see the future, they only did so by saying that God showed them what was to come. No one shows God anything about what will happen in the future, because He is already there.

The reason He seems to be silent, is because He is patiently waiting, not willing that any perish, but that all come to repentance.

Thank God that He hasn't left us guessing as to where on the time scale we are in these "last days." He has given one sign that brings to culmination all these signs. This we will look at in the next chapter.

Chapter Eleven
The Prophetic Sign

All of these signs were have looked at are merely a forerunner of one final prophecy preceding the Second Coming of the Lord of Glory, the Messiah-- Jesus Christ. The skeptics who say that these signs have always been with us are right. To a degree, there have always been earthquakes, rebellious youth, famines, etc., but the sign to look for was the Israeli occupation of Jerusalem (Luke 21:20). The degree heated up in 1967.

Way back in 1860, when the Suez Canal opened, the United Kingdom gained better seaborne access to its important possession of India. Their borders were becoming increasingly threatened by the southward expansion of imperial Russia. Britain, by intervention in Egypt and by a treaty with the small

Sheikhdoms of the Arabian Peninsula, made a number of alliances to guarantee the safety of its sea routes. With the collapse of the Ottoman Empire following the end of World War I, the occupying European powers carved up the area under a mandate system established by the League of Nations.

In 1920, it authorized Great Britain to set up a postwar government in Iraq. Britain drew the new country's boundaries according to its strategic needs, mostly around old Ottoman provinces. The foreign presence rallied the Iraqis, and awakened a sense of national pride that would eventually drive the British from Iraq.

After the end of World War II, thousands of Jews began to pour into Palestine. Zionists had pushed for the creation of a Jewish homeland there for many years. However, Palestinian Arabs resented the new settlers, and there began a friction which eventually caused the United Nations to propose dividing the British mandate of Palestine into separate Arab and Jewish states. Arabs strongly opposed the plan, but in 1948 when Great Britain withdrew because of high costs in policing that state, among other things, Israel declared itself a state. It was front page news. *The New York Times* carried the headline:

"ZIONISTS PROCLAIM NEW STATE OF
ISRAEL...The Jews Rejoice."

Then on Thursday, June 8th, 1967, the newspaper announced what those who knew their Bible's had been waiting for for years--the Israeli possession of Jerusalem:

"ISRAELIS ROUT THE ARABS APPROACH SUEZ, BREAK BLOCKADE, OCCUPY OLD JERUSALEM...**Israelis Weep and Prayed Beside the Wailing Wall.** Israeli troops wept and prayed

Israel police guard arrested Palestinians in Jerusalem. The Bible warns that in the latter days Jerusalem will be a "burdensome stone" for all people (Zechariah 12:3).

today at the foot of the Wailing Wall--the last remnant of Solomon's Second Temple and the object of pilgrimage by Jews throughout the centuries.

"In battle dress and still carrying their weapons, they gathered at the base of the sand-colored wall and sang *Haltel*, a series of prayers reserved for occasions of great joy. They were repeating a tradition that goes back 2,000 years that has been denied Israeli Jews since 1948, when the first of three wars with the Arabs ended in this area. This wall is all that remains of the Second temple, built in the 10th century before Christ and destroyed by the Romans in A.D. 70.

"The Israelis, trembling with emotion, bowed vigorously from the waist as they chanted psalms in a lusty chorus. Most had sub-machine guns slung over their shoulders and several held bazookas as they prayed. Among the leaders to pray at the wall was Major General Moshe Dayan, the new Defense Minister. He told reporters, 'We have returned to the holiest of our holy places, never to depart from it again.'"

To many it was of little real significance, but to Bible scholars around the world it was of tremendous importance. The Jewish people, after over

1900 years without a homeland, occupied Israel. In 1967, *they set foot in Jerusalem fulfilling the words of Jesus Christ spoken 2,000 years earlier.*

God warned that if the Jews forsook His Law, He would scatter them throughout the earth, allowing them to be put to shame, then draw them back to Israel. The Bible makes special reference to Jews being drawn back to Israel from "the north country" (Jeremiah 23:7-8). The nation of Israel is the night-light on the clock of Bible prophecy. It shows us how close we are to the "midnight hour." David Ben-Gurion, the first prime minister and minister of defense in Israel made this statement:

"Ezekiel 37 has been fulfilled, and the nation Israel is hearing the footsteps of the Messiah."

Prophet's Predictions

The signs of the times are so obvious, even casual students of the Bible can see that the Second Coming of Jesus Christ is near. Look at these words from an occult book I have quoted from earlier in this publication:

"Centuries before the great exile of the Jewish people more than 1900 years ago, Moses, Ezekiel, Jeremiah, Isaiah and others foretold that the Jews

171

would be thrown out of their homeland to be dogged by privation and persecution. The expression 'wondering Jew' was apt:

And the Lord shall scatter thee among all people, from one end of the earth even unto the other...And among those nations shalt thou find no ease, neither shall the sole of thy foot have rest. (Deuteronomy 28:64-65)

"As surely as the prophets predicted the Jew's dispersion, they forecast their return. Ezekiel's words were fulfilled on May 14, 1948, when the State of Israel was established in Palestine:

For I will take you from among the heathen, and gather you out of all countries, and will bring you into your own land. (Ezekiel 36:24)" (*Predictions*, Fisher and Commins, Van Nostrand Reinhold Company--Prophecies (occult sciences) page 21.

Chapter Twelve
Pure Prophetic
Waters

Early Christians found everlasting life without having to acknowledge that the Bible as we know it, was supernatural. The New Testament wasn't even compiled when the Gospel was given. People couldn't read. There was no such thing as the printing press. They weren't converted because they intellectually accepted that the Bible was God-inspired, they merely acknowledged they were sinners and called upon the name of Jesus Christ, the Savior. They heard the *spoken* message and believed it.

We are even more fortunate than they, because we have the testimony of prophecy and all the other evidences to help us see that the Bible *is* God-breathed. This should help humanity believe and embrace the Gospel of salvation. But sadly, they would rather drink cheap wine from the empty skull of a dead prophet, rather than taste the pure waters of prophecy from the Word of God. Look at the difference between the vague predictions of Nostradamus (minus his biblical plagiarism), and those of the Word of God. Napoleon was right when he said, "Man will believe anything, as long as it's not in the Bible."

Nostradamus originally fled to Italy because the remark he made about the virgin Mary sounded very much like that espoused by Protestants. Protestants were called "protest-ants" because they protested against the doctrines of the mother church. This movement originated when a devout Roman Catholic monk named Martin Luther read in the Bible, that salvation came by "faith," and not by what he "did." He had always been under the assumption that he had to become "righteous" by the reciting of prayers, confession, taking the sacraments, etc. But in the Scriptures he read verses such as:

"For by grace you are saved through faith, and that not of yourselves. It is the gift of God, not of works, least any man boast" (Ephesians 2:8-9).

Not only did those who read the Bible find that the Scriptures taught that salvation was the free gif

174

of God, but they found that it said that the "virgin" Mary they worshipped had at least five more children after she had Jesus (Matthew 13:55). They understood that she was most blessed because she bore the Messiah, but they denied that she was the Virgin Mother who ascended to Heaven and was to be prayed to. These Roman Catholics protested because they found that the Scriptures said that a believer could have *direct* and personal access to God, not needing the intermediary ministry of Mary or that of a priest (1 Timothy 2:5). Other revelations from the Word of God came thick and fast. They saw that Peter, whom they were taught was the first pope, flatly refused homage of any sort (Acts 10:26), and that he was actually married (Matthew 8:14).

They protested when they discovered that Roman Catholic authorities had removed the Second of the Ten Commandments. They erased the Commandment given to Moses which forbad the bowing down to any image of any likeness "of things on the earth or things in Heaven" (Exodus 20:4-6). They saw that the Roman church had then split the Tenth in two to replace it. They also discovered that the Bible doesn't even hint of a place called Purgatory, let alone the common practice of paying indulgences to priests to get people out of such a vicinity.

They *protested*, and millions of God-loving believers lost their lives purely because they believed the Word of God. Their blood was spilled because of their testimony of the truth. As prophesied of a thousand years earlier in Holy Scripture, they were "slain for the Word of God and for the testimony they held" (Revelation 6:10).

Are You Good Enough?

In the light of all the evidence we have looked at, the question we should be asking is, *How may you and I obtain eternal salvation?* *Everything* else fades in the light of such a profound question. The way to find this out is to ask ourselves if we have obeyed the Ten Commandments. Most would answer the question, "Well I've broken one or two, but nothing too serious, like murder, etc." So, let's go through them and see how you do:

1. "You shall have no other gods before Me." Is God first in your life? Do you love God above all else? Many years ago I purchased a television set for our children, but the first evening we had it, I arrived home from work and found that they didn't even bother to greet me. They were too busy watching cartoons. I turned it off and explained to them that if they ignored me because they preferred

to watch television they were setting their love on the *gift* rather than the *giver*. That is a wrong order of affections. In the same way, if we love anything, husband, wife, children or even our own lives-- more than we love God, we are setting our affection on the gift rather than the Giver. This is a transgression of the First Commandment. In fact, the Bible says that we should so love God that our love for Mom and Dad and brother and sister should seem like hatred compared to the love we have for the God who gave those loved-ones to us.

We are also *commanded* to love our neighbor as much as we love ourselves. Jesus spoke of a Samaritan who found an injured stranger, bathed his wounds, carried him to an inn, gave money for his care and told the inn-keeper that he would pay for his expenses. We call him the *good* Samaritan, but in reality he wasn't "good" at all, he merely obeyed the basic command to love his neighbor as himself. That is a picture of how God expects us to love our fellow human beings. We should love them as much as we love ourselves...whether they be friend or foe.

Have you loved God with all your heart? Have you loved humanity as much as you love yourself? Most of us have trouble loving our "loved" ones. You be the judge. Will you be innocent or guilty on

Judgment Day of breaking that Commandment? *I'm not judging you*--I'm asking you to judge yourself before the Day of Judgment, so that you can get off the road before the big-rig comes. If you refuse to acknowledge that you are on the highway of sin, then you will not get off. Sentence for transgression of the First Commandment is death.

2. "You shall not make for yourself any graven image."

This means that we shouldn't make a god to suit ourselves, either with our hands or our mind. I was guilty of this. I made a god to suit myself. My god didn't mind a "white" lie or a fib here and there--in fact, he didn't have *any* moral dictates. But in truth my god didn't exist. He was a figment of my imagination, an "image" which I shaped to suit myself. Is your God the One revealed in Holy Scripture? If not, then you have made your own god to suit yourself--you have committed the oldest sin in the Book; you are guilty of breaking the Second Commandment, and scripture warns that no idolater will enter the Kingdom of Heaven.

3. "You shall not take the name of the Lord your God in vain."

Have you ever taken God's name in vain-- substituted it for a four-lettered filth word used to express disgust? Hitler's name wasn't despised enough to use as a curse word. God gave you every pleasure you have ever known, and if you have used His holy name in that manner, you are a blasphemer and will not enter the Kingdom of God.

4. "Remember the Sabbath Day, to keep it holy."

I ignored this command for 22 years. Even though God gave me the gift of life, never once did I ask what He required of me, let alone set aside one day in seven to rest. I was guilty of breaking this Commandment.

5. "Honor your father and your mother."

Have you *always* honored your parents in a way that's pleasing in the sight of God? Ask Him to remind you of the sins of your youth. You may have forgotten them, but God hasn't.

6. "You shall not murder."

Jesus warned that if we get angry without cause we are in danger of judgment. If we hate our brother, God calls us a murderer (1 John 3:15). We can violate God's Law by attitude and intent.

7. "You shall not commit adultery."

Who of us can say that we are pure of heart? Jesus warned, "You have heard that it was said to those of old, 'You shall not commit adultery.' But I say to you that whoever looks at a woman to lust after her has committed adultery already with her in his

heart." Remember that God has seen every thought
you have had and every sin you have ever committed. The day will come when you have to face His
Law, and we are told that the impure, fornicators
(those who have sex before marriage), and adulter-
ers, will not enter the Kingdom of God. Punishment
for transgression of this Commandment is the death
penalty.

  8. "You shall not steal."
Have you ever taken something that belonged to
someone else (irrespective of its value)? Then you
are a thief--you cannot enter God's Kingdom, you
have violated His Law.

  9. "You shall not bear false witness."
Have you ever told a lie? Then you are a liar. How
many lies do you have to tell to be a liar? Just one.
The Bible warns that *all* liars will have their part in
the Lake of Fire. You may not think deceitfulness
is a serious sin. God does.

  10. "You shall not covet."
That means we shouldn't desire anything that
belongs to another person. The covetous will not
inherit the Kingdom of God.

  Who of us can say we are not guilty of breaking
these Commandments? *All* of us have sinned, and
just as with civil law, you don't have to break ten
laws to be a law-breaker, so the Bible warns, "For

whoever shall keep the whole Law, and yet stumble in one point, he is guilty of all."

A little girl was watching a sheep eat grass and thought how white it looked against the green background. But when it began to snow she thought, "That sheep now looks *dirty* against the white snow!" It was the same sheep, but with a different background. When we compare ourselves to the background of *man's* standard we look pretty clean, but when we compare ourselves to the pure snow-white righteousness of *God's* standard--His Law, we can see ourselves in truth, that we are unclean in His sight. That Law is the holy standard by which humanity will be judged on Judgment Day.

This may sound strange, but the worst thing you could do at this point of time is to try and clean up your lifestyle--you realize that you have sinned, so from now on you will keep the Ten Commandments, do good deeds, say the right things and think only pure thoughts. But should a judge let a murderer go because he says he will now live a good life? No, he's in debt to justice and therefore must be punished.

The Law of God is merely like a mirror--all a mirror does is show you the truth. If you see egg on your face, you don't try and wash yourself with the mirror, its purpose should be to send you to water for cleansing. Neither should you try and wash yourself with the mirror of God's Law...that's not the purpose of the Ten Commandments.

The sight in the mirror is not a pretty one, but if you don't face it and acknowledge that you are unclean, then all that "dirt" will be presented on Judgment Day as evidence of your guilt, and then it will be too late to be cleansed.

Perhaps you think that God is good and will therefore overlook your sins. But if you were guilty of terrible crimes in a civil court and said to the judge, "Judge, I am guilty but I believe that you are a good man and will therefore overlook my crimes," the judge would probably respond by saying, "You are right about one thing; I am a good man, and it's *because of my goodness* that I am going to see that justice is done, that you are punished for your crimes." The very thing that many people are hoping will save them on Judgment Day, God's "goodness," will be the very thing that will condemn them. If God is good, He *should* punish murderers, liars, thieves, etc., and Hell will be their dreadful fate.

What a terrible place Hell must be. If you saw in the newspaper that a man received a $5 fine for a crime, you could conclude that his crime was insignificant. But if a man received *multiple* life sentences, you could conclude that his crime was heinous. In the same way, we can catch a glimpse of how terrible sin must be in the sight of God by looking to the punishment given for it--*eternal* punishment. Sinful, rebellious, ungrateful humanity never bothered to thank God for His blessings of kindness, color, light, food, warmth, joy, beauty, love and laughter so He will take it all back from them. Instead of showing their gratitude by obedience to His will, they used His name to curse and mocked His Word. Take the time to read what Jesus said Hell was like in the Book of Matthew. I am afraid for you...please, look honestly into the mirror of the Law, then seek the "water" that cleanses every sin.

Am I your enemy because I have told you the truth about Hell? If you don't believe what I am saying about it, it means you think God is corrupt (that He hasn't the moral backbone to seek justice), that Jesus was a liar, that the Apostles were false witnesses, that God's promises in His holy Word are nothing but prefabricated lies, and there is no greater insult to God than to call Him a liar. By doing so, you are *adding* to your transgressions.

Imagine if you reject the Savior, die in your sins and find that what I have told you is the Gospel truth? Then it will be too late, you will be judged for your sins. If that happens, and your eyes meet my eyes on the Day of Judgment, I'm free from your blood. I have told you the truth, but if you choose to ignore it your blood will be upon your own head...you will have no one to blame but yourself.

Can you see your predicament? You are guilty of sinning against God Himself, and because you have a conscience, you sinned "with knowledge." Isn't it true that every time you lied, stole, lusted, etc., you did it *with knowledge* that it was wrong? On the Day of wrath you will be without excuse. Many times the Bible warns that God will see that justice is done. If there is no punishment for murder, then God is unjust. He would be like a corrupt judge who turns a "blind eye" to the dealings of the mafia.

Does the fact that you have sinned against God scare you? It should. You have actually *angered* Him by your sin. The Bible says His wrath abides on you, that you are an "enemy of God in your mind through wicked works." But let fear work for your good in the same way that a fear of jumping out of a plane at a great height would make you put on a parachute. Let your will to live open your heart to the Gospel of salvation.

The Secrets of Nostradamus Exposed

In late December of 1995, a dog named Chocolate fell into the icy waters of the Calgary River in Alberta, Canada, after it was spooked by a passing train. As the terrified dog struggled vainly to climb out of the freezing waters, rescuers, knowing that the dog could only live for a few minutes, got in a boat and rushed to rescue the distressed animal.

As they reached the now exhausted dog, a man reached his out loving arms. But as he did so, *he was viciously bitten on the face by the dog that he was trying to save*. Of course, we can excuse the animal by saying that it was panicked, and therefore not in its right mind. In its desperation to save itself, it didn't realize that there was another trying to save it. Learn a lesson from a dog. God is not willing that you should perish. You are sinking into the icy waters of death. Don't try and save yourself. Don't panic. Stop the struggle, and let God pull you out. That is called "grace."

To make clear what an incredible thing He has already done for you, let's look again to civil law. You are standing in front of a judge, guilty of *very* serious crimes. All the evidence has been presented and there is no doubt about your guilt. The fine for your crime is $250,000 or imprisonment. However, you haven't two cents to rub together. The judge is about to pass sentence...he lifts his gavel, *when someone you don't even know steps in and pays the fine for you.* The moment you accept that payment, you are free to go. Justice has been served, the law has been satisfied, and what's more, the stranger who paid your fine showed how much he cares for you. His payment was evidence of his love.

That's what God did for us...in the person of Jesus Christ. We are guilty but He paid the fine 2,000 years ago. *It is that simple.* The Bible puts it this way: "He was bruised for our iniquities...Christ has redeemed us from the curse of the Law being made a curse for us...God commended His love toward us, in that while we were yet sinners, Christ died for us."

It was no small thing for Jesus to die for us. The only thing that would satisfy the demands of Eternal Law was the *suffering* death of the sinless Son of God. *What love God must have for us!* He suffered an agonizing death, so that you wouldn't have to be punished for your sins. His sacrificial death and resurrection means that you need no longer be in debt to the Law, and God can now grant you everlasting life if you obey Him. Death no longer has a legal hold upon those who belong to Jesus Christ.

Plane Motive

Two men were offered a parachute while seated in a plane. The first man was told it would improve his flight, but the second man was informed that he had to make a 25,000 foot jump. When the flight struck severe turbulence the first man took his parachute off because, as far as he was concerned it didn't improve the flight. But during the same violent turbulence, the second man clung tighter to his parachute...and even looked forward to the jump.

Each man's *motive* for putting the parachute on determined whether or not he would keep it on. In the same way, the *reason* you should "put on the Lord Jesus Christ" shouldn't be to find peace, joy, and true happiness. Neither should it be to have your marriage healed or your problems fixed, etc. (to have your flight improved), but it should be to escape the jump to come. You have to pass through the door of death. Then, when the flight gets bumpy (when problems come) you won't fall away from the faith. The pure motive for coming to God should be to ask for His mercy, because you have sinned against Him.

Today, not Tomorrow

In the 20 years it took for airbags to move from the drawing board until they were a reality in motor vehicles, an estimated 500,000 people lost their lives through accidents. What a terrible waste of human life. Once their potential was realized, they should have been installed in new vehicles immediately, but instigation took time and money.

It will not cost you one penny to be saved from a head-on collision with Eternal Justice. It was all paid for 2,000 years ago. The time side however, depends on you. How long will you wait? How long have you got? The god of this world blinded your mind for years, so don't put your eternal salvation off for another moment.

What then should you do? Simply repent and put your trust in Jesus Christ as your Savior and Lord. Think of a man who has committed adultery. His faithful wife is more than willing to take him back, so what is the attitude in which he should approach her? It should be one of tremendous humility, asking for forgiveness, and determining in his heart never to *even think* of committing adultery again. That's how you should approach God.

Just in Case

I was in a store in Baltimore, Maryland, when I saw something that caught my eye. It was what looked like a genuine but dud hand grenade, mounted on a plaque which said, "Complaints--pull a number." The number was through the pin on the hand grenade. It was an ideal gift for a friend, so I purchased it and put it in my hotel room.

I didn't give the thing any more thought until I went to put it into my suitcase just before leaving for the airport. I decided not to put it in the case, just in case it was x-rayed and I wasn't there to explain that it was fake. Instead, I put it into my carry-on bag.

When I approached the security metal detectors, I couldn't help but remember how terrorists favored a hand grenade in the hand to get things done in a hijacking. If anyone jumped them, the grenade would fall from their hand and go off in seconds. So it was an effective terrorist bargaining device.

If I put my bag on the x-ray belt and it went through, they would see the outline of a metal hand grenade, and before I knew it, I would probably find myself on the ground with a few guns pointed my way.

I therefore quietly said to a uniformed attendant, "Excuse me. I have a small problem, can you help me?" Then, trying to sound as un-terroristic as possible, I meekly said, "Have you ever seen those fake...ar...imitation, ar...novelty...ar...pretending

189

hand grenades on a plaque--*Complaints: pull, take a tag*?" He smiled and said, "Yeah. I have one at home." I sighed with relief. When I told him that I had one in my bag, he asked for it and took it to show to his boss.

His boss wasn't as congenial. His face dropped to a dealing with a difficult passenger expression, and he told me that there was no way they could let it through. I would have to take it back to the counter and check it in. What's more, I was to keep anyone from seeing it as I did so. He then said that he didn't think they would let it go through with my baggage.

I had previously given the lady who checked me in a small gift, so she gladly checked it in. However, I was expecting a welcoming party when I arrived at Los Angeles airport.

If you are not yet saved, you are holding a hand grenade with the pin pulled out. Don't wait until tomorrow to make peace with God. Please, do it now.

The Rush

You've always wanted to sky dive, but the thought scared you too much to try it. That is, until you met someone who had made over 100 jumps. He talked you into it by explaining how safe it was.

His enthusiasm was contagious. He spoke of the freedom of falling through the air...the adrenalin rush...the unspeakable exhilaration.

Now you are standing on the edge of a plane, looking down upon the earth far, far below. Everything had been checked. *Double* checked. This was safer than driving on the freeway. That helped deal with the fear. Modern parachutes are state-of-the-art. Besides, there is a back-up 'chute. Still, your heart is beating with apprehension.

Suddenly, *you jump*! You have trained so much for this moment, you instinctively spread your hands and legs. The speed is unbelievable. The power of the air forcing itself against your body is incredible. It's like a dream. Your are defying the law of gravity, racing through the air at more than 120 m.p.h.!

The earth is looming closer. All normal sense of time lost. Speed, thrust of air, unspeakable joy. You glance at the altimeter on your wrist. Only another ten seconds and you will pull the cord and feel the jolt of the parachute opening. All that you had been told was true. The adrenalin rush is like nothing you have experienced. If only it could last a little longer. Reluctantly, you pull the cord. It opens, *but there is no jolt!*

You tilt your head back to see a sight that

horrifies you. The parachute has twisted and is trailing like a flapping streamer. Your heart races with fear, and pounds in your chest. Your eyes bulge in terror. Your chest heaves as you gasp for air. You try and keep a clear mind and remember your training...pull the second cord. *Nothing happens!* You pull again. Again! Harder. *Harder!* Nothing. Your body lets out a scream, a groan of panic. Your heart is pounding even harder. Faster. Sweat breaks through your skin. A thousand thoughts speed through your mind. Your family! Your fate! ...Safer than driving on the freeway! You whisper, "What a fool I was...to think that I could defy the law of gravity." Now a merciless law waits for the moment of impact. The ground accelerates towards you. No words can describe the terror gripping your mind. A voice is speaking to you. It is the voice of good sense. It is the voice you ignored so often: "You *have* played the fool. You have given up your life...your most precious possession for a cheap thrill. You have exchanged your loved ones for a rush of adrenalin. What a fool...what a fool!"

One word stands alone to describe how you feel about what you have done. One word screams within the corridors of your terrified mind as the earth races towards you...as death readies to embrace you. One word. A word that you have never understood fully until this moment in time. That terrible word is "Remorse!"

The world the flesh and the devil whisper to you about how pleasurable sin is. God isn't angry at sin. God is love. It is safe to jump into the arms of iniquity and abandon yourself to a free fall through its vast domain.

You go where angels fear to tread. But it is worth it. The rush is everything sin promised. You drink in iniquity like water. You love the darkness. Conscience speaks again and again, but you ignored its warning. You are defying the Moral Law, and loving every minute.

Now you stand before the Judge on Judgment Day. You pull your first line by telling God what a good person you are. Nothing happens. The Moral Law rushes at you. In panic, you pull the second line and tell God that you believed in Him. *Again, nothing happens*. It is no use. Your mouth is stopped. The Moral Law accelerates towards you even faster, promising to so impact you, it will "grind you to powder." Death and Hell wait to embrace you. Unspeakable terror fills your heart. Conscience speaks so clearly now: "What a fool you have been. You rejected the mercy of God in Jesus Christ. You have given up your loved ones in exchange for the joys of a sinful lifestyle. You relinquished your most precious possession, *your very life* for the cheap thrill of sin. What a fool! What a fool!" One word will stay with you for eternity. One word alone will echo forever within your tormented mind. *Remorse!* You whisper the word, "Remorse...remorse."

Suddenly you are staring at the ceiling of your bedroom, still mouthing the word through dry lips. *Remorse!* The sheets are wet with sweat. *It was just a dream.* You look out the window and see the sun breaking through the green trees. It was just a dream! It's morning now. A peaceful new day. Today's the day you go sky diving. It will be your first time.

A Second Look

Late into the afternoon of Wednesday, December 20, 1995, a woman and her daughter rushed to catch a flight from New York to Miami. Even though the flight was delayed by two hours because of snow, the congestion caused them to miss it, and consequently the connecting flight to Colombia. The woman no doubt looked at the small plaque connected to her key ring which said, "Lord, help me to have the serenity to accept the things I cannot change..." and felt a deep sense of frustration that they had missed the plane to Miami.

Later that night, they learned that the plane they were supposed to be on had smashed into a mountain just 13 miles from the airport, killing 160 passengers. I am sure that the plaque she held in her hand had a different meaning to her after she was saved from such a terrible death.

Those who have faith in Jesus Christ look on the Bible in a different way than how they looked upon it before were saved. No longer is it merely a history book, or even a book of incredible prophecies which have come to pass. It is a *living* Book. It is a Book of "exceeding great and precious promises." It is a Book that provides comfort. It is a road map, a guide, a light in the darkness, and it points to Him who is the fulfillment of all its wonderful promises--Jesus Christ, the only-begotten Son of God, who saved us from the wrath which is to come.

If the many prophecies of Nostradamus are true and many are yet to be fulfilled, those who believe them are left in a dilemma of what they should do. He left them in a boat on the Niagara River without a paddle. Nostradamus gave no instructions to his believers.

Not so with the message of the Bible. All its

wonderful prophecies were given to bring us to a place of eternal security. If you are still not sure what you should now do to be saved, merely bow your head, confess your sins to God and determine to turn from them. Read Psalm 51 and make it your own psalm--your personal prayer. Then put your faith in Jesus Christ, in the same way you would put your faith in an elevator. You don't just "believe" it will lift you up, you actually trust yourself to it. Once you have made peace with God, read the Bible daily and obey what you read. If you do that, you will never go wrong, and God will never let you down.

As long as you trust and obey God I can predict your future with more certainty than tomorrow's sunrise:

"The path of the just is as the shining light, that shines more and more unto the perfect day." (Proverbs 4:18)

"Eye has not see, nor ear heard, nor have entered into the heart of man the things which God has prepared for those who love Him." (1 Corinthians 2:9)

Please remember to pray for millions who are deceived by the occult. To them it is but a harmless and fascinating lifestyle. They don't realize their true state before God...nor their future:

"Now the works of the flesh are evident...adultery, fornication...idolatry, sorcery...those who practice such things will not inherit the Kingdom of God." (Galatians 5:19-21)

"...and they did not repent of their murders or their sorceries or their sexual immorality or their thefts." (Revelation 9:21)

"But...murderers, sexually immoral, sorcerers, idolaters and all liars shall have their part in the lake which burns with fire and brimstone which is the second death." (Revelation 21:8)

* * *

Thank you for taking the time to read this book. If you have found this publication helpful, feel free to call us for a complete list of other books, tracts, videos and tapes by Ray Comfort:

1(800) 437 1893 credit card orders,
phone (310) 920 8431,
fax (310) 920 2103

or write to:

Living Waters Publications
P.O. Box 1172
Bellflower, CA 90706.

This publication is available at 40% discount if you purchase 10 copies or more. You may like to consider buying copies and giving them to friends.

Purchase the powerful video "The Secrets of Nostradamus Exposed" ($20 plus $3 S/H) and we will give you two FREE copies of this book to give to friends (just mention this "special" when you write or call). This documentary exposes the secrets of Nostradamus in a persuasive visual medium.